GW00702233

DOVER

Collected Memories
of a Century

DOVER
Collected Memories of a Century

A. F. 'Budge' ADAMS

and

MERRIL LILLEY

TRIANGLE PUBLICATIONS
DOVER

iv

Published by
Triangle Publications, Dover
© to individual contributors

1st Published 2000

2nd Print 2003

ISBN 0-9539478-0-7

Typeset in Veljovic Book
by a member of the Dover Society

Printed in Great Britain by
A. R. Adams & Sons (Printers) Ltd
Dover

PREFACE

THE FIRST meeting of the Dover Society was held on 25th April, 1988 and the first issue of its *Newsletter* appeared in June 1988. Over the years the publication included various themes, one of the most popular being a collection of memories of Dover, mostly from members of the Society but a few from other sources.

For the year 2000 it was decided to collect together and publish in one volume all the articles and reminiscences of the twentieth century from the *Newsletters*. These range from childhood memories of the first decade of the century to more recent events like the discovery and preservation of the Bronze Age Boat and, to end the century, the Lantern procession and Mardi Gras Carnival of the New Year celebrations on 31st December 1999 and 1st January 2000.

To help the reader the book is divided into five parts, or themes:

Part One, called *The Golden Triangle*, consists of a series of articles written by 'Budge' Adams. These appeared in several early *Newsletters* and describe Dover as it was in the first half of the century. As many of the places described in *The Golden Triangle* are referred to in writings which follow in other sections, it was felt to be appropriate to start with this and to give it a section of its own.

Part Two includes very early memories of Dover before the First World War and also covers the war years 1914-18. Part Three has a wide selection of writing about the years between the wars and Part Four deals with the Second World War, 1939-1945. Some contributions cover incidents which could be placed in more than one section of the book and where this occurs the pieces have been placed at the end of sections where the reader can see that the narrative flows on to the following part.

Part Five is devoted to the second half of the century, ending with accounts of the beginning of the new millennium in Dover. This section differs from the other four in style and content. One reason for this is that when members wrote about their memories of Dover they tended to choose very early memories and most of these belonged in the first four sections of the book. Articles written about events in the second half of the century tended to be more factual and less personal. Therefore, it was decided to select topics which had been reported in the *Newletter,* were the recollections of members and had some relevance to the work of the Society.

The book is a joint production. The choice of material, editing and the linking and introductory sections have been the work of Merril Lilley and the page-setting, lay-out and choice of presentation have been the work of 'Budge' Adams.

At all stages of planning and production the compilers have been grateful for the advice and guidance of Derek Leach, who has kept a watchful eye on the work from the beginning.

CONTENTS

PART 1

THE GOLDEN TRIANGLE

in the Early 1900s

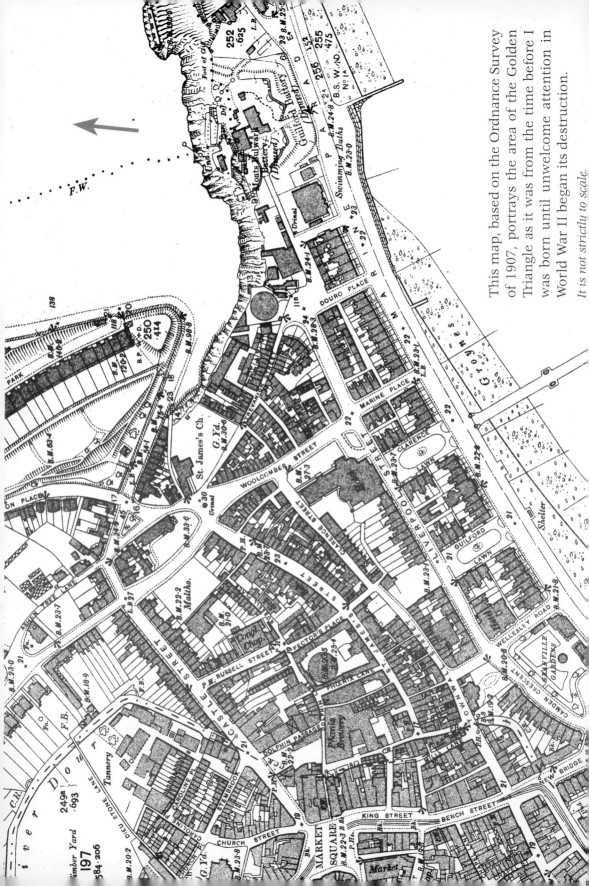

This map, based on the Ordnance Survey of 1907, portrays the area of the Golden Triangle as it was from the time before I was born until unwelcome attention in World War II began its destruction.

It is not strictly to scale.

THE 'GOLDEN' TRIANGLE

A. F. 'Budge' ADAMS

NO, NOT IN AND AROUND NORTHERN THAILAND and beyond, but in Dover. It is, in fact, *My* Golden Triangle and is that part of the town that grew on the land reclaimed, partly by man and partly by nature, from the old harbour between the East and the West Brooks and was bounded by a line running roughly from the Rifles' Monument (in what is becoming known as Camden Square), via Bench Street, King Street and Church Street to the bridge in Dieu Stone Lane and then on through Ashen Tree Lane and Trevanion Street to Boundary Groyne, at that time still known to me, and to all those who lived in the area, as Castle Jetty.[1]

The Burlington Hotel in all its pristine splendour. The grandest building in the Golden Triangle.

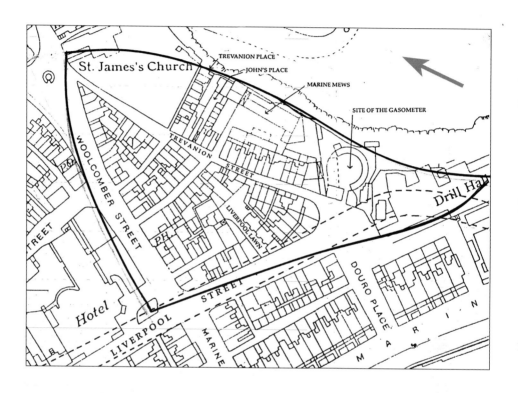

The Woolcomber Triangle is defined by the heavy black line and the parallel dashed lines indicate the route of the present Townwall Street, i.e. the A20.

THE 'WOOLCOMBER' TRIANGLE

I N 1903 MY FATHER MOVED into 37 Castle Street where, in 1909, I was born, and where, excepting the years 1913-15, I lived until I was 27. By 1936, it was evident that more space was needed to bring up the family and we moved out to Crabble Hill. However, my love affair with Castle Street[2] and the little area that I define as the "Woolcomber Triangle", continued and now spans more than ninety fascinating years.

The area seethed with life and activity. Old St. James's Church, the present day Sports Centre and the former filling station at the seaward end of Woolcomber Street, and Woolcomber Street itself, define the 'The Woolcomber Triangle', where now not a single person lives, but where there were, prior to 1939, 103 separate dwellings and a population

The 'Woolcomber Triangle' in the 1920s. The Dovor (sic) Gas Company's first production site and gasometer can be seen at centre right. At centre left, covered by trees, is Old St. James's Churchyard, where now is the car park for the leisure centre.

6   certainly not less than 450^3, but about 545 if the occupants of the fifty-two flats into which the Burlington Hotel had been converted are included. This density was typical of the down-town areas at the time and the people's daily needs were provided for by many small shops and enter-

Lamidey's – gentlemen's hairdresser in Woolcomber Street

prises. Throughout my teens, on the south-western side of Woolcomber Street, roughly where, in 1998 Thompson's Garage was demolished and turned into a surface car park, there was a furrier's establishment – hardly necessary for anyone's daily needs! – and a butcher's shop, a large and very formally conducted men's hairdressing saloon, with revolving hair brushes, driven by a system of belts and pulleys powered by a small boy in the basement – later replaced by an electric motor, – a grocer's shop – the International Stores – a post office, Offredi's sweetshop[4], and, on the corner with Clarence Street, a wool shop which itself was the successor to a herbalist. Then came the Burlington Hotel, which though nominally in Liverpool Street, had a greater frontage in Woolcomber Street. It was not then used as an hotel but provided accommodation for the Burlington High School, for fifty-two flats, for a baker and for an 'elite' ladies' hairdressing establishment.

In the picture on the page opposite, Exhibition Place can be seen on the eastern side of Woolcomber Street, which runs upwards and left from bottom centre.

On the other side of the street, from Old St James's Church toward the sea, was an almost continuous parade of shops. First were three small cottages: in one lived a watchmaker and in another a well-known local figure, Mr Henry Epps, who invariably wore a frock coat with a silver watch chain looped across his waistcoat. He was, I think, the Chief Clerk at the Dover Gas Company. The meticulous timing of his twice daily walk via Castle Street to his office in Biggin Street enabled my parents to say to me, 'Off to school, quickly, Mr Epps has gone by!' Shops and a public house stood side by side almost until Liverpool Street was reached.

There was, in a section defined by a large decorative plaque on the frontage as 'Exhibition Place', a greengrocer, a bookie, a decorator and a confectioner and then, reverting to the name 'Woolcomber Street', there was a boot repairer, another hairdresser, a general stores and on the northern corner of Trevanion Lane leading through to Trevanion Street, a tobacconist and newsagent.

Beyond the lane was a couple of dwelling houses, a drug store and the Imperial Dairy. Here was Woolcomber Lane, which also led through to Trevanion Street. Hopper's Bakery stood on the lane's eastern corner, and

Part of the Woolcomber Triangle, c 1946. The White Horse Inn and Old St. James's Church are left of centre. The scrub that grew during the war – at the right of the church – obscures the old cemetery. Exhibition Place is just left of bottom centre.

8   then, continuing, came the *Mail Packet Inn,* a greengrocer's shop and, in a mews behind the houses and reached by another narrow lane, the Marine Garage. This was operated by the well-known Gibbs family, and, before the 1914 war was used by the same family as mews and stables for their hackney carriages and phaetons. On the seaward side of this lane was a confectioner's shop which I remember as the place where my father would, throughout much of my early boyhood on our Sunday morning walk to the Sea Front, treat me to a glass of sarsaparilla at a cost that equalled my total week's pocket money, 2d.

Next to this shop, in a building with a frontage curving in a perfect quadrant into Liverpool Street, and which, in 1861 housed the Dover Collegium, was a watchmaker friend of my father, George Maton, a very clever craftsman with a well-deserved reputation for good work, and recognised all over East Kent. (see picture on page 3.)

Close under the cliffs where now is built the present-day Sports Centre was Trevanion Street and there lived many whose business or calling was connected with the sea, mostly boatmen or fishermen. 'Trevanion' is the name of a man who came to Dover in the first half of the 18th century, became the Member of Parliament from 1744 to 1792 and did much for the town. He lived in 'Trevanion House' at the eastern end of the street and, dying in 1810, was buried in St. James's Church.

In the 1920s, on the northern side of this ancient street the first fifty metres were taken up by the low boundary wall of St James's Churchyard and then a terrace of seven small houses, Trevanion Place, running at 90° to the cliff, faced the eastern boundary of the churchyard. A little further on was John's Place, a tiny courtyard behind the street frontage, also running up to the cliff face and entered through a 'tunnel', no more than a metre wide, cut through the ground floor of Nos. 3 and 4. Just beyond this courtyard was the entrance to Trevanion Mews – livery stables – in an extensive area behind the houses. The Mews was a maze of caves under Castle Hill and included a horse hospital and stabling for many working horses. Beyond that was a public house, the *Star and Garter* and then a few houses further on, at the end of the street, were the premises of a wood and coal merchant named Wellsted. His business was conducted from a new 'Trevanion House' built in the late 1850s on the site of John Trevanion's original house and adjacent to which, from 1822 until 1855, when the Company moved to Union Road (Coombe Valley Road), was the producing plant for the Dovor (*sic*) Gas Company. Old pictures show a gasometer on the site – still there until the first reconstruction of the A20 – and when Townwall Street was being extended to join up with the Sea Front at East Cliff there could be seen, in the excavations, some

of the original mains piping that, fortunately, I was able to photograph.
The road works also revealed the flat chalk surface at the foot of the cliffs, ribbed by the action of the waves and covered with centuries of accumulated detritus. (It is believed that this 'platform' was used in the 18th century and earlier, when the tides were suitable, as a road to and from Deal – with a similar one on the western side of the bay to and from Folkestone – for wagons that could be pulled by two horses, which, had the steep inland roads been used, would have required the power of four or six.)[5]

Throughout my childhood and early teens road traffic was light; it contributed to the life of the area and did not dominate or destroy as it does today. Drivers said 'Hello' or passed the time of day with pedestrians who were certainly not considered to be obstructions to the free flow of potentially lethal vehicles. In the early 1920s traffic lights had not yet been installed and policemen were stationed at three stretegic points – the Worthington Street–Biggin Street junction, the top of Snargate Street and at the Castle Street–Maison Dieu Road junction – to control the traffic. They stood in the middle of the road and by hand and arm signals controlled the traffic flow. Originally they had nothing to attract the eye of road users to the signals made by their hands or arms but they were very soon issued with white gloves and not long after that they were given white oversleeves extending from wrist to elbow – and all was well. On a sunny summer day they appeared to be quite happy but on wet days and in the winter the situation was very different. In the winter or in wet weather they wore waterproof capes and on point duty – as it was called – on a wet day in the winter, with the rain running off his helmet and finally cascading off his cape, a point duty policeman looked miserable and dejected. Drivers obeyed the signals, which they regarded as reasonable – the habit of 'jumping the lights' or its equivalent had by then not evolved.

CASTLE STREET
and its
WESTERN ENVIRONS

IT IS NOT EASY for present day Dovorians to accept the fact that the actual road surface of Castle Street was formed on the top of an embankment specially built across a low lying and well-watered meadow used for centuries to fatten cattle and sheep – across, in fact, the flood plain of the river – and that the foundations for the houses, which have semi-basements, were laid at the level of the fields the road crossed. But that is an established fact, corroborated by the bald legal phrases of deeds and leases drawn up when there were changes in the ownership of land or hereditaments. In the 17th and 18th centuries the meadow was owned by Kent's Quaker community and the income derived from it was used to support its indigent members. Later it was owned in three separate parcels by two local men and the Trustees of the Dover Almshouses[6] and later still, in 1835 it was acquired by a local consortium of developers. The new owners' first task was to bridge the river which ran across the meadow land from the east side of the present Kwik-Save site and on to St. James's Lane in front of the multi-storey car park. When the site of the 'Snoops' night club - until recently 'Images' - was developed into Leney's cask yard (and more than 100 years later into the Granada Cinema) the river, as it approached Castle Street was set into a conduit and came out into the open again a little upstream of the footbridge over the river at the junction of Dolphin and St. James's Lanes. At that time Dolphin Lane continued on to open into the Market Square between Killick & Back's drapers' shop and Binfield's the wine merchants (approximately where now is the entrance to Creighton House).

In the 18th century and until the building of Castle Street, Eastbrook Place was a rural footpath which continued across the meadow to St. James's Street. At the junction of Ashen Tree Lane with Dieu Stone Lane and Charlton Back Lane – in 1862 to be transformed into Maison Dieu Road – the open space was known as Horsepool Sole, within the bounds of

12 Horsepool Ward. From the Sole[7] to the sea the route was via Ashen Tree Lane to the bottom of Laureston place, then bearing right, into St. James's Street. (At that time the present day road to Deal and beyond did not exist, it was carved out of the slopes below the Castle *circa* 1792.) After crossing the face of Old St. James's Church one bore left into Trevanion Street, very roughly parallel with Woolcomber Street, and thence on to the ropewalk and herring-hang on the foreshore above high water mark where now the latest edition of the A20 runs in front of the houses in East Cliff.

Castle Street was designed to run from Ashen Tree Lane southwest toward the Market Square and the carriage-way was, in fact, an embank-

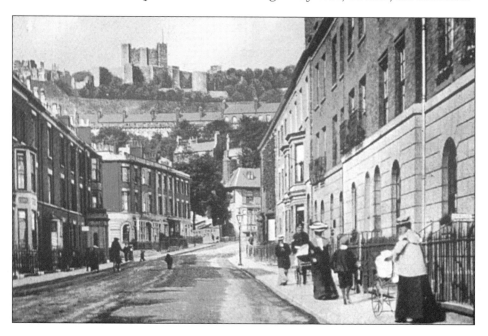

Castle Street in 1905 - four years before I was born at No. 37.

ment built across the meadow from Ashen Tree Lane to Stembrook, high enough at the sou'western end to align with the top of the arched bridge built over the river. The final stretch, from Stembrook to the Market Square, was built some few years later, after action, not entirely unfamiliar to us today, was taken in an attempt to force the owners concerned to accept the Paving Commission's offer of £1,500 for the buildings and land necessary for the scheme. The Commission applied to Parliament for powers of an early form of compulsory purchase and though the Bill was approved and the new street opened up to the Market Square by 1837, the total cost to the Commission was more than the planned expenditure.

Eastbrook Place (and Castle Place, a logical continuation from the seaward side of Castle Street to St. James's Street), was part of the narrow,
insignificant, Charlton Back Lane. When the proposals for the new Castle
Street became known it was decided to widen this lane as a general
improvement to the area and to provide further sites for the speculative
building that was proposed. The builders adhered to their plan to begin
Castle Street at Ashen Tree Lane but they grasped the opportunity to
enhance the aspect of the proposed properties above the new intersection. Three graceful houses, Nos. 1, 3 and 5, built on the northwest side
can be seen today, but those opposite, equally elegant and with pillared

'Castle Terrace', a name in use in 1871 but now 1, 3 and 5 Castle Street. Immaculately preserved by its present owners, the colour of the painting is the only discernible difference.

porches, similar to what is now, I believe, 2 Castle Hill Road, were
demolished for road widening in two phases, in 1904 and 1936.

Building in Castle Street began in 1835 or '36. The foundations of the
houses were laid at the level of the original meadow, the lower floor being
a semi-basement, fairly deep at the front, i.e., below the level of the
embankment, but shallower on the garden face at the rear. It is interesting
to note that at about half a metre below the surface of the gardens of Nos.
27 to 43, running out to the river at the rear, is a bed of shingle that may
well have formed the shore line in Saxon times. (This I discovered as a

14 boy when digging graves for departed and lamented pets, and which, for reasons of public health, my father insisted should be very deep) I do recall one grave I dug so deeply that it met the water table – the river was very near.). The new road across the fields, which in its essentials lasted until 1921 was constructed of water-bound macadam and was built with an extremely high camber, the centre being almost half a metre above the gutter level.I verified this in 1921 when, at the remaking of the road after the damage caused by World War I motor traffic, the camber was reduced to its present level and Castle Street then became Dover's first tar-macadamised thoroughfare. The reduction of the road's camber to about one third of a metre was the maximum possible because, after the road works, the cable for the 100 volt electricity supply to the South Foreland Lighthouse, the Eastern Arm of the harbour and the Southern Breakwater, which ran along the centre of the street, was then at the minimum depth the law allowed.

The five-fold increase in the town's population during the 19th century meant that most of the new houses in Castle Street were immediately occupied by doctors, dentists, solicitors and veterinary surgeons (of which latter there were many, all over the town, as are garages and car repair shops today) whilst the remainder were principally used as lodging or boarding establishment.

In Castle Street in my childhood and early teens there were, on the NW side, a dentist, a doctor, three firms of solicitors, two builders, an estate agent, a dairy, the Registrar for Births and Deaths for the St. James's Sub-District, a cycle and perambulator dealer, a confectioner's shop and a corn and seed merchant. At the southern corner of Stembrook were the offices of Elwin & Lambert, solicitors who doubled as the legal and administrative side of the then embryonic Dover Rural District Council. Next a downward flight of steps led to a row of small cottages behind the street frontage and at

Penn's 'Military Furnishers' shop at the corner of Castle Street and Stembrook in 1908. By 1912 it was Knocker, Elwin & Lambert, Solicitors. Now the Council Offices occupy the site.

90° to it. There was another access to this small area via a narrow arched roofed "tunnel" between the ground floors of two cottages on the SW side of Stembrook. Next to and above the steps in Castle Street was the shop of Mr Hesse, a German taxidermist. Next came a hairdresser, Mr Packham's photographic studio and a small cul-de-sac, Shakespeare Place, in which were two houses and a single storey building that, in 1909 when I was born, and for some time later, was the long-established printing works of Mr 'Snatcher' Smeeth. His retail shop premises were later taken over by Mr Packham. On the SW corner of Shakespeare Place was a bar and back entrance to the Burlington Inn, the main frontage being in Church Street. The premises of G. W. Chandler, plumber, and decorator were next and when his business failed in the early 30s, his whole family decamped to Lydden Spout where for five or six years they lived in some tents on the foreshore. Next to Chandler's was Florence Igglesden's most exclusive milliner's shop, then a tiny tobacconist's shop and finally, and most well-known of all, the Umbrella Shop of the bearded Mr Hubbard, where now is the wide pavement in front of the Trustee Savings Bank, and which, incidentally, was the last local building to be destroyed by enemy action.

In the early years of this century on much of the site of the superstore, now in the hands of Somerfield, its third owners, was Brace's Flour Mill, taller than any other building in Castle Street and covered with white-

Castle Street at Stembrook circa 1920. The tall white building at L. is Brace's Mill.

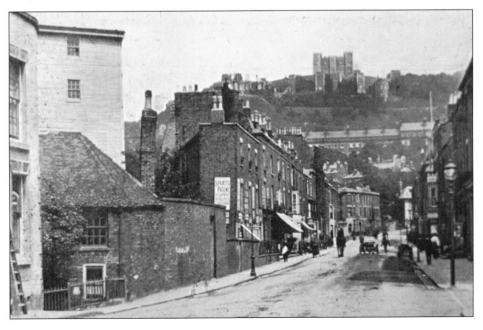

16 painted horizontal lap-boarding. The remains of the brickwork supporting the bearings of the mill's power source, a water wheel, may be seen to this day in the river just before it disappears under Castle Street.

No. 27, now occupied by the architects, Dudley Marsh, was the home and offices of the Terson family, the founders of the present-day house and property agents who were originally in part of No. 27 but who now also occupy No. 29. The stocky figure of Thomas Achee Terson, irreverently known to the children of the area, for very obvious reasons, as "Red-faced Terson," daily could be seen, bowler hatted and with two inches of stiff white cuffs and a high white collar prominent against a dark formal

Castle Street in 1914. 'Riverside House' at left. covered with a red-leafed creeper.

suit, striding purposefully down the street, intent on a deal perhaps, and we children were in awe of him. No. 27, known as "Riverside" is large and double-fronted and from my childhood until some time in the 1950s was entirely covered by a striking red-leaved creeper that obliterated all and every architectural feature. At leaf fall in the autumn the street was deeply carpeted with purple-red leaves and the building, and another, No. 16, diagonally across the street and similarly covered, still remained cloaked, though perhaps a little more thinly, in the brilliant creeper.

I have a distinct memory, as quite a small child, of the spreading of straw in the road, between Nos. 17 and 33 approximately, to cushion the sound of traffic passing the house of someone who was extremely ill, though I cannot now recall for whose comfort this was done.

No. 37, exactly opposite Russell Street, was the base from which, in my childhood and early teens, I explored the "Golden Triangle", my territory, that I am now attempting to describe. Even in the dark, or blindfolded (part of a game we used to play), I would know where I was by the sound of my footfall on the many kinds of pavement, (or do I imagine it?), from the ambient noises of particular streets or lanes. The smells from the brewery, the malthouses, the corn chandlers' and coal merchants' stores, the stables, the hotel kitchens, the public houses, the nostalgic sweet-sour smell of a water-bound road sprayed in summer from a water cart to lay the dust and, yes, the smell of the 'gents' in Woolcomber Street and behind the Sea Baths, all played their part and helped to make me, and my peers, know and feel that we were an integral part, not only of the life, but of the sticks and stones, the bricks and mortar, of that most interesting part of the town. That feeling remains with me to this day, though, alas and sadly, there is very little left to enthuse about.

On the seaward side of the street at the corner with Maison Dieu Road, on the site until recently occupied by the M.F.I. store, were two interesting establishments: Webber & Son, watchmakers and gunsmiths (Webber's son - I forget his name – was a member of the Bisley 100) and the piano and musical instrument warehouse of Mr Douglas Robb, where, al-

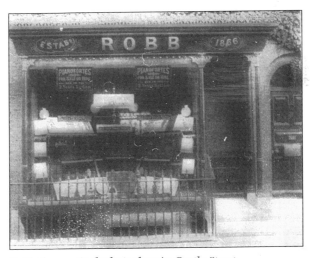

Robb the music dealer's shop in Castle Street.

most always, a grand piano dominated the front showroom. Mr Robb had died some years previously and the business was conducted by Mr Wright, a kind and gentle man who had some disability in his left leg. The architects, Fry & Miller and later Knocker, Elwin & Lambert, solicitors, were in the double-fronted house now occupied by the Solitaire computer firm and which was, at that time, covered with the same type of red-leaved creeper as was the Terson house nearly opposite. Next, at No. 18, was the Castle Creamery where, in 1931, my very new wife would, for 6d (2 1/2p) buy a pint of sour cream for the making of a rather good Hungarian soup.

At No. 20 were the offices of the Castle Concrete Company, founded by Capt. Noble who lived in Victoria Park and which produced concrete and breeze blocks on the late nineteenth and early twentieth century tanyard site over which has been built Pencester Court and the super-market.

From this firm grew the builders' merchant's business operated in the chalk pit between Tower Street and Priory Hill and later to become a constituent part of the firm of Castle Harris, with the late George Marsh as the manager. A little lower down, at No. 28, Mrs Skinner conducted Pettitt's Commercial College, and most of the town's aspiring shorthand-typists and secretaries were her pupils, my sister amongst them. The slightly eccentric Mr Skinner bought, sold and repaired typewriters, but his pride and joy was a large open tourer motor car to which he had fixed, at the four corners, poles almost a couple of metres high and which supported a wide green canvas sheet stretched tightly across them. Many years later, in India, I was reminded – I do not know why – of Mr Skinner's car when I saw basically similar though much more ornate canopies on elephants used in ceremonial processions. The Skinners, in and about 1914, were part of the compulsive migration from Snargate Street that had begun in the latter years of the last century and finally stripped all glamour from the town's erstwhile main street.

Mowll's, the solicitors, were very early occupants of Nos. 34 and 36 - possibly the first. I have a grateful memory of John Mowll, an enormously tall man, proportionately broad and heavy, who extracted my arm when I, aged eleven, had foolishly wedged it in the grating of the gutter drain outside his office. The solution to my problem was really very simple: Mr Mowll sent one of his clerks for a bucket of cold water which he poured over my arm and wrist and then, grasping me under the armpit, he pulled with all the considerable force of which he was capable – he was a big man and well over six feet in height – and I was free!. It hurt a bit but the damage was slight and I was happy to have escaped so relatively easily and with my hand, miraculously, still attached!. I am reminded by the memory of this incident that Mowll's strongroom in the basement was used, during the last war, as an effective and very handy air-raid shelter into which many of those living or working nearby would dive when shell or air raid warnings were sounded.

On the opposite corner of Russell Street, Cross's stationer's shop was, prior to 1914, the 'Victoria Hotel and Billiard Saloon' and was, amongst other things, the headquarters of the Dover Cycling Club, a very well-supported and active organisation. The premises were built expressly as an hotel, it being thought by the developers that Russell Street would be continued onward as a new thoroughfare to the Sea Front and that the site would have great potential. Property owners in Fector's Place and St.

James's Street were not co-operative and the extension was never built.
High up on the Russell Street frontage one can, though now with some
difficulty, discern the words "Victoria Hotel" in large black lettering painted
on the brickwork. At No. 42, next door but one, a stockbroker had his
offices and then, at No. 46 was Mr G. J. Carter, the Superintendent Registrar of Births and Deaths for the entire Dover District. At that time No. 46
had a plain unadorned frontage but in 1930 I watched the fitting of the
rather elaborate bow window which now graces it. No only did I see the
window installed but I watched its construction by the father of my cur-
rent inamorata. Next was Pepper's the old established butcher's shop, now
a take-away food place, and then there was Miss Norah Murch the milliner, whose elegant premises were later 'antiqued' by Mr Gibbs and became his 'Old Curiosity Shop' and, subsequently, a solicitor's office. The
bearded Mr Forster, who was succeeded in my time by Mr E. G. Sharp, had
a chemist's shop where now is Blake's Wine Bar and he also did business
as a mineral water manufacturer. Most small town chemists, as a sideline,
made and sold mineral waters by retail and one could always buy a bottle
of mineral water and drink it in the shop from a glass the chemist would
provide. On the walls of the chemist's shop and also on the terrace of
shops opposite there were a number of brightly painted advertisement

Easte's shop and stores in Castle Street. (The present day carpet store is at L of the tall building).

panels. Brockman, the cycle dealer's and Easte, the corn chandler's were particularly striking.Next to Forster's, where lately was the auto spare-parts shop, was the showrooms of the Dover Motor Company, with work-shops in the factory in the rear. Originally this building had been occupied by E. Hills & Sons, coach builders and specialist coach painters who for many years did the painting and lining of the Daimler bodies that were made by Palmer & Son at Cherry Tree Avenue and at the foot of Coombe Valley Road, in premises originally a brewery and now occupied by a large block of retirement flats. In the large rooms above Hill's showrooms were Cresswell & Newman, architects, surveyors and civil engineers and where now is the restaurant known as Dino's was another butcher's shop. Previous to Dino's occupation and subsequent to their amalgamation with Leney & Co. the premises were used by Fremlins, the brewers, as their local offices. The impressive building on the corner of Dolphin Passage was built as the offices of Alfred Leney & Co., proprietors of the extensive Phœnix Brewery on the site of the St. James's Lane multi-storey car park. The firm worked closely with Flint & Co. – a family connection – and between them they operated well over 200 tied houses in East Kent. The offices, which were originally stone-faced, were badly damaged during the last war and were rebuilt in brick to the original design and all the present-day dimensions and features are as first conceived. When the Leneys ceased to brew in Dover, at the time of their amalgamation with Fremlins, the offices were taken over by P. Hawksfield & Son, an old-established local firm of coal merchants who moved from their offices at the corner of Fector's Place and St. James's Street. Hawksfield's business was, later, absorbed into the Powell Duffryn Group and was operated by Corrals. In 1989, the premises were occupied by a bookmaker and a shipping and forwarding agency and occupancy has changed since then.

Mr Peter Hawksfield, Alfred Leney & Co. and the Dover Harbour Board became, in 1903, my father's first printing customers. Hawksfield's and Leney's continued with us until their extinction but in 1992, 89 years later, we still had the pleasure of printing the Harbour Board's 'Port News'.

During the 1914-18 War Leney's offices were the focus of very consider-able interest on the part of the townspeople. In each of the two windows on the Castle Street frontage were fitted large sloping boards covered with green baize and every day, as copies were received, telegrams from the War Office and other sources giving the principal news of the moment (or rather the news that the War Office allowed to be known), were posted. There were, sometimes, telegrams advising next-of-kin that their serving relatives had been killed or were missing in action and I think these must have been handed in by local people, possibly as a convenient means by

which to advise friends or relatives of the bad news. I do recall the tears
and anguish of those first made aware, in the windows of those offices in
Castle Street, of the loss of friends or relations. On the other side of
Dolphin Passage, where now is "Images", previously the famous Granada
Cinema, with Mr Sydney Sale as manager, was Leney's coopers' yard, where
barrels were made and repaired. The cask-yard produced a distinctive smell
from the beer-soaked barrels, the new timber for staves and the black-
smith's forge where the barrel hoops were formed and shaped. The barrels
were smoothed with a particularly heavy type of spokeshave and the shavings were inches deep in some parts of the yard. (I am fortunate to possess
one of the spokeshavers from this yard.) The entrance to the yard from
Castle Street was through a pair of large wrought-iron gates beneath a
similar arch surmounted by a big brightly gilded figure of a phœnix standing
in a leaping fire with wings outstretched. On the apex of the high pointed
roof of the brewery in Dolphin Lane was an even larger gilded phœnix
that was covered with canvas during the 1914-18 war when its use as an
aiming or ranging point by enemy gunners and airmen became obvious.
After that war it was re-gilded and remained high on the roof , as I recall,
until the next war began, when, to the best of my recollection it was removed, never again to be replaced. The brewery, on the site of the present
multi-storey car park, was severely bombed and later demolished.

Next to the yard and moving on towards the Market Square, was a confectioner's shop above which were the auction sale rooms of Flashman &
Co. The sale rooms extended over part of the Antwerp Garage, owned by
the Dover Motor Company who operated a taxi business under the management of Mr Lou 'Broncho' Gearing, a daring and flamboyant driver of
the firm's Model T Fords. Mr Gearing earned his sobriquet, so it was said,
when he rounded the corner of Castle Street into the Market Square and
Cannon Street at more than 40 miles an hour on two wheels and sounding
his horn, in a dash to the Royal Victoria Hospital with a man who had
been involved in an accident on Castle Hill. Next was a small tobacconist's
shop and then the return frontage of Flashman's big shop occupied the
last fifty or sixty metres of the street

When the lower part of Castle Street was formed it cut diagonally across
plots of land that had frontages in Church Street and this is the reason for
the peculiar shapes of the ground plans of the buildings in Castle Street
which were, in fact, built on or utilized the gardens behind the houses in
Church Street. The *Burlington Inn* and others in Church Street seized the
opportunity to extend their premises to provide frontages on the new street
and the odd shape of the Antwerp Garage was because it was adapted
from the outbuildings of the Antwerp Mews based in Church Street.

Another area, distinctly different, and formed around Church Street, Stembrook and Caroline Place, well known to me in the minutest detail in the 1920s because many of my friends lived there, lies on the western side of Castle Street, beyond the river Dour. The east side of Church Street, though damaged, was not destroyed during the war but in the years 1948 to 1950, to facilitate redevelopment, all the buildings in the area were razed to the ground.

The hub or focal point of the area that, as the Roman harbour silted up, became the flood plain of the river, was at the minor crossroads behind St. Mary's Church from which radiated, clockwise from the NE., Caroline Place, Stembrook, Church Street and Church Place. Caroline Place, until demolition, was an L-shaped cul-de-sac, its short leg leading out from the cross roads and the longer turning right, towards the river. It is very probable that Stembrook also was originally a cul-de-sac with the river at its blank end. The present upward slope at the eastern end – much steeper before 1948 or '50 - was formed, probably in 1884 to '35, to give accrss to Castle Street, the new thoroughfare then under construction, at the level of the newly made bridge. Stembrook Cottage, almost exactly where now is the entrance to the Carpet Store, was built on the new slope.

Thinking of Stembrook first, on the left from Castle Street, where now are the gates into a private car park for Stembrook Court, stood the *Ancient Druids* public house. Demolished during redevelopment, the licence was transferred to the new *Roman Quay* at the junction of Stembrok and Church Street. There were nine little houses on the SW side and a tunnel-like entrance, in the centre of the nine, led to two small houses in the rear, on the site of the car park just mentioned.

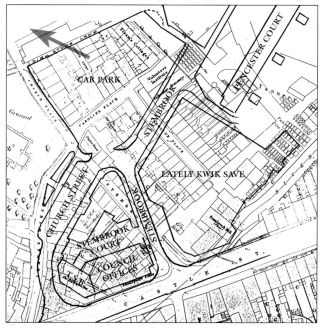

The reconstruction of lower Castle Street and the Stembrook area, drawn over a pre-war map.

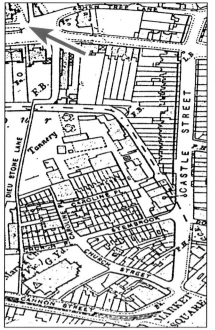

Map of the area circa 1910

Flashman's war-damaged workshop in Dieu Stone Lane. (see next page)

On the same side, *c.*1936, were two 23 small general shops, one owned by Mr George Le Grys and the other, much better stocked, and incredibly efficiently run by the Walker family. Between them lived a Mr Walter Lyus and as a boy I often wondered – and still do – why two men with such interesting and unusual names lived in adjoining houses and, indeed, whence they came. Wilson's shop was tucked in behind the last house in Church Street, which, curving round from the bottom of Castle Street, finished half a metre into the road width of Stembrook. This appears to be a rum piece of planning, excusable, perhaps, because no planning, in the modern sense, was done in the early 19th century.

On the NE. side, on the slope from Castle Street, Stembrook Cottage, with a tiny garden in front, was next to the entrance to Brace's Mill and to Bacon's tanyard. The mill had been demol-ished by the early 1930s and soon after the tanyard closed down, the pits were filled in and the buildings were used by the Castle Concrete Co. for the production of breeze or concrete blocks.

On the other side of the entrance, at a right-angle to the road, was a row of three tiny dwellings. At the corner where Stembrook met Caroline Place, was the workshop and stores for the Corporation Water-works distribution network. Next to the workshop was a yard used as a builder's store and beyond it, at the turn of the century, was the *Old Fountain Inn,* in my time occupied as a private dwelling. Then there were two or three small store-places before Caroline Place, with twenty-one houses on its longer leg, turned to the right.

24   At the angle in CarolinePlace and facing the eastern end of St. Mary's Church were, in my youth, two buildings, used as a store and 'garage' for its barrows by Partington's Kent Bill-posting Company. I clearly recall seeing the men folding, on huge tables, 8-sheet Double Crown posters, ready to be posted on the numerous sites in many East Kent towns.

In the 80s or 90s of the last century the buildings housed the Gordon Boys' Orphanage, later moved to its more well-known place in St. James's Street at the northern corner of today's *County Hotel.*

At the time when my father was a proud member of the Royal Cinque Ports Volunteers, (a Victorian version of a territorial army), Partington's

The Church Street-Stembrook 'hub'. Directly ahead is the spire of New St. James's Church.

two buildings were respectively the Volunteer Institute and the Volunteer Armoury. When the premises were no longer needed by the Volunteers, Mr E. Morgan, later the manager of Partington's, formed the Boy Messenger Brigade whose members would deliver notes (and parcels) anywhere in the town, a most useful service in the days before the telephone. My last memory of those places, before the war whisked me away, was that Hedgecock Warner & Co. used them as furniture showrooms.

On the NW side of the short leg were two dwelling houses, several indifferent small store places, and a tall bill-hoarding, three storeys high, as

I recall, on the blank wall of a store. It was a source of perpetual amazement to me that the bill-posters could, with a bucket of paste, a long-han-
dled brush and a huge shoulder bag in which the folded sheets of the 8-
sheet posters were stowed in correct order, climb a tall ladder and do their
tricky job at a height of eight or nine metres.

Church Place had a row of eight tall, unpretentious but pleasant houses
facing St. Mary's Church and each had a forecourt with steps leading down
ro a semi-basement. At the end of Church Place, on the other side of Dieu
Stone Lane and lying parallel with.it, was Flashman's cabinet makers' and
upholsterers' workshop and on the ground floor their undertaking
department. Further to the NE along Dieu Stone Lane were Church Court
and Elsam's Cottages, two more culs-de-sac, but regrettably they are not
so clear in my memory that I can describe them accurately.

Church Street, running as it still does today, from Castle Street to the
NW end of Stembrook, was much narrower than it is now, but the buildings on the Cannon Street side are substantially the same as they were
eighty years ago. At the corner with Castle Street, where now is LloydsTSB,
was Hubbard's, the umbrella shop, much previously Laslett's livery
stables and then with frontages lazily wheeling round to Stembrook was a
hairdresser's, the *Burlington Inn,* a private house, two shops, one dealing
with 'wireless' components and battery charging and the other with fish
and chips. Then followed two more private houses and Farley-Woodhams's
Central Dairy, the biggest private dairy in the town.

A house or two came next and then there was the *Star Inn,* whose
proprietor, early in this century, was the enormous Mr Langley who
weighed, I believe I am correct, 302 kilos (48 stone!). It was said that to get
him into bed he had a derrick installed, with double-sheaved blocks and a
leather sling. Using this his wife could then easily hoist him up and,
presumably, drop him in the appointed spot!

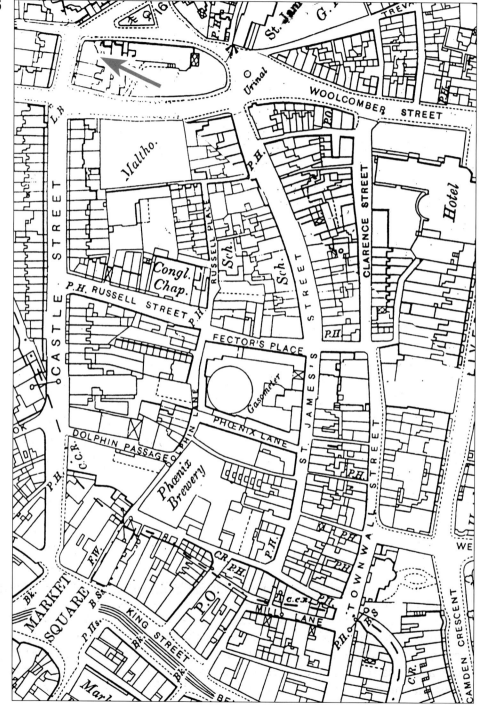

CASTLE STREET
and its
EASTERN ENVIRONS

THIS PART OF THE GOLDEN TRIANGLE, that is, Russell Place, Dolphin Lane, St. James's Street, Townwall Street and Liverpool, Street is covered reasonably well on the map on the opposite page and excluding Liverpool Street, which is much more recent it can be seen that its dominant road pattern, NE to SW is a perpetuation of the area's 16th century road axis which ran in a flat curve, inclining a little towards the sea, from the then Deal road, now Laureston Place, via St. James's Street and Queen Street to Cowgate, at that time the town's portal on the southwest side. (Elizabeth I on her peregrination of Kent is reputed to have entered Dover through Cowgate and then proceeded down a hill later to become k nown as Queen Street but in the sixteenth and seventeenth centuries commonly referred to as 'The King's Highway'.[8] It is said that when the Queen's train was entering Dover the wagons at the tail were still toiling up Folkestone Hill.[9])

Clockwise from Castle Street, in Castle Place[10] (in the 1860s embraced in Maison Dieu Road) was the distribution depôt of the British Oxygen Company – extensive premises entirely filling the space between the rear of 12 Castle Street[11] and the Elizabethan houses near the top of St. James's Street where was, originally, an enormous malt house with access from both Golden Cross Passage and Castle Place, which was later replaced by two courtyards, both with ten small houses on each side and called, collectively, Castle Place. I am not sure when the Castle Place courtyards were demolished, possibly when Maison Dieu Road was extended in the 1860s, but the area was free and waiting for development when the British Oxygen Company decided to build a depôt there early in the 1900s. Sometime in the 1920s the Oxygen Company's premises were taken over by Southern Autos, part of John Dodd's 'Southern' empire and re-vamped into car sales showrooms and maintenance workshops. Fifteen to twenty years ago (I cannot be certain as to the date) the site was cleared and the inelegant and now unoccupied M.F.I. building was erected in its place.

28   The garage's workshops, behind the street frontage, were originally a large malthouse with access from both Golden Cross Passage and Castle Place and were part of the Leney's Phœnix Brewery and Leney's Table Waters complex.

Opposite, on the NE side, just into Castle Place, was the Imperial Photographic Studio, later to become W. Martin's, the electrician's shop and later still a café and eventually an electricity sub-station was built there. On the site of the present vehicle hire depôt was the walled garden of Castle Hill House where, at the age of twelve, in the loft of a coach-house, my friend Charlie Hopcroft and I experimented with a twenty-packet of Player's cigarettes and I began my career as a heavy smoker (ceasing, however, in 1980). The garden was eventually built over and occupied by Rowland's wholesale grocery business. Later, when the firm moved to St. Radigund's Road, the warehouse was destroyed and replaced by a petrol filling station, later to become a vehicle hire depôt. In the now demolished part of the curved wall at the seaward end of the garden was a large stone in which was carved the date '1666', reputed to have once marked the site of St. Helen's Gate, or tower, part of the town wall and sited at, approximately, the junction of Fox Passage with St. James's Street. In the latter part of the 18th century Mr Phineas Stringer, who commissioned the building of Castle Hill House, had rescued this stone and caused it to be built into the wall surrounding his garden. When the wall was being demol-

ished, and, as no other person appeared to be interested, I made frantic efforts to obtain custody of the stone. Arrangements were made with the architect, the contractors and the secretary of the owners of Castle Hill House, for me to be present at 8.30

A rendering of Fred Kennet's water colour of The White Horse Inn, Old St. James's Church, 'The Ornament' and at extreme L, the wall.

on a certain morning to collect and take the stone away for preservation. At 8.30, when I arrived, the bulldozer had finished its work, the wall was demolished – how similar to the Brook House affair – and I was able to find only three small bits of the actual stone, which sadly, showed no ev- idence of the date carved into it; they are still, I hope, under a hedge in my garden – just small pieces of stone – completely useless. Thus are vital bits of Dover's history lost for all time.

Just seaward of this wall, in the centre of an area now much diminished by the entrance to the Sports Centre car park, was an elegant circular cast-iron pissotière surrounded by cast-iron railings and a dense privet hedge. A number of people living in the immediate area were concerned that this Victorian relic should be preserved but, alas, it very conveniently disappeared, as a result, we were told, of a misinterpretation of instructions (!) just prior to alterations to the road layout.

The *White Horse Inn* and St. James's Old Church are both in St. James's Street, a reminder of the time when neither Castle Place nor Woolcomber Street existed as thoroughfares. Castle Hill Road, often referred to as Castle Hill - which it is not - is comparatively recent, having been built in the 1790s. Castle Hill and Claremont Place ran from a point opposite the *White Horse* across the face of Castle Hill House, to the top of Castle Street where, on the seaward side, all the houses have long since been demolished. St. James's Street ran SW from the *White Horse* to St. James's Lane and was, in my youth, the artery of a lively community. Opposite the still remaining houses, Nos. 5, 7 and 9, at Nos. 4 and 6, were the offices

Nos 5, 7 and 9. Early 17th century houses at the top of St. James's Street.

of Stilwell & Harby, the solicitors, who are now in Maison Dieu Road. The lower numbered buildings and St. James's Rectory which stood facing north-west almost exactly where now is the entrance to the Sports Centre car park, had disappeared many years earlier in two separate stages of road widening. Next to Stilwell's was Betts, the greengrocer's shop, which,

St. James's Street in the early 1900s.

with two similar shops in Woolcomber Street, (not in the same ownership) effectively supplied the area's needs. That is not strictly true because, on Tuesdays and Fridays, Mr Betts toured the streets with his cart piled high with fruit and vegetables and most of those who lived within the Golden Triangle bought their needs, quite literally, on the doorstep. Every year Mr Betts with his horse and cart were at St. James's Sunday School Treat in Old Park, which was later transformed into an extensive military barracks and which, still later, became redundant and were disposed of the area is now being re-developed. I was one of the children who were given marvellously long rides up and down the length of the park at a penny a go.

Next to Betts shop was Arthur's Place, a narrow lane with a terrace of cottages on the NE. side: on the SW side was the Assembly Gospel Hall which doubled back and had another entrance a few doors down in St. James's Street. Beyond the Gospel Hall there was a tiny courtyard

with three houses, one each side and one facing the entrance. Most of the
houses in Arthur's Place were occupied by boatmen, some were entrepreneurs providing the beach pleasure boats and others formed the crews of the many motor boats that shipped and landed the North Sea Pilots.

On the eastern side, between the Assembly Hall and Fector's Place – who remembers where that was? – were two or three general shops, a bookbinder, a wholesale stationer, a goodly number of excellent and varied craftsmen amongst whom was Mr Cole, previously a lifeboatman – in the days when the lifeboat was an oared vessel – who taught me to sail an Essex One Design and who, after my father's death, very largely took over the rôle of father to me and of grand-father to my older daughter.

On the other side and next to the still existing houses at the top of the street, was the *Golden Cross* public house,[12] an opening into Russell Place called Golden Cross Passage, and, on the other side of the passage-way, Johnson's most comprehensive general shop. As well as the requirements of our elders, Johnson's sold tiger nuts, horse beans, liquorice root, liquorice straps and pipes, catapult elastic, toy pistols and the 'ammunition', called 'caps', for them, water pistols, air gun pellets, marbles, toffee apples and all the other absolute necessities for a young boy's life. Continuing towards the SW and next door to Johnson's was St. James's Parish Hall, where the awe-inspiring Miss Stratton, previously a missionary in Africa, was the Superintendent. A few doors away was St. James's Girls' School with Miss Clipsham as the headmistress and a

The Russell Place area, now almost entirely car park.

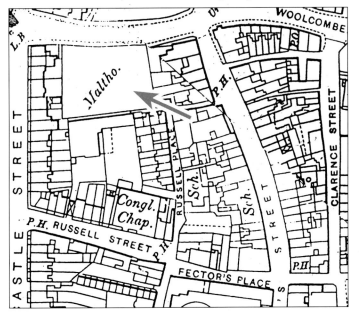

little further on was the intersection with Fector's Place and Fox Passage which formed a 'natural break' between the two halves of the street.

Reverting to Golden Cross Passage: half-way along it and facing into Russell Place was Golden Cross Cottage with a large gilded cross, a metre or more high, planted on the wall above the front door. Beyond Russell Place, in an extension of Golden Cross Passage towards Castle Street, was a terrace of small three-storied houses – if one counts the basement, entirely below ground level, – entered by a steep flight of steps and in most cases used as the living quarters. This little lane also gave access to the malthouse mentioned earlier.

Until the lengthening of Russell Street, which brought about the annihilation of Fector's Place and the destruction of another piece of Dover's history, the tiny piece of road that led, opposite the *Castle Inn,* into the car park, was the last remaining vestige of Russell Place, where, in my time as a boy there was St. James's Boys' School and St. James's Gymnasium and Men's Club. Behind the readily visible three-storied houses on almost the entire NW side there was an 'invisible' courtyard with six or seven houses approached by a narrow 'tunnel' about a metre wide, apparently bored through the ground floor room of one of the houses and whereby that particular room was made very small. Right opposite was St. James's Gymnasium, the home of the 9th Dover Scouts; for five years I was a member – happy memories – and with them I learnt so much. Later, after it became the parish social club, the building was destroyed by a bomb. I did have but, regrettably, do not still have, a photograph of the interior after the bombing and amongst the rubble, at a drunken 45°, is one of the billiard tables.

Next to the Gymnasium there were four very small cottages, with two ground-floor rooms and a minute bedroom wedged into the roof. Then came St. James's Boys' School with a tiny yard attached to it, and next to that, and very much larger, was the coal yard of Peter Hawksfield & Sons. Square in the middle of the carriage way of the relatively recent extension of Russell Street was the site of a house that faced toward Castle Street and where lived Hawksfield's yard foreman. When Hawksfield's moved to Union Quay, Mr James, a coal dealer whose premises were at the bottom of Queen Street, took over the yard, bought the house and therein installed his son, who had earlier acted as chauffeur to Mrs Beresford Baker of Prospect House.

From the *Castle Inn* to St. James's Street the comparatively narrow thoroughfare was, and had been for 150 years or so, known as Fector's Place, leading on, through Fox Passage to Townwall Street. In 1939 it was still lined, on the NE side with Fector's original warehouses and there was, at the corner with St. James's Street, a building which in the 1890s, had housed a velocipede manufacturer, but which, from 1900 to the early '30s was occupied by Peter Hawksfield & Son. In 1931 or '32 Hawksfield's moved their coal yard to a wharf on Union Quay (now almost always referred to as Union Street) and their offices into recently vacated premises at the Castle Street junction with Dolphin Passage. The office in St. James's Street was almost immediately occupied by the local branch of the National Union of Mineworkers.

Peter Fector, whose warehouses were built and first occupied about 150 years ago in an originally unnamed cul-de-sac running NW out of St. James's Street towards the meadows over which Castle Street and Russell Street were built – later, and logically, to become known as Fector's Place, – was a nephew of Isaac Minet, a Hugenot who, after the Revocation of the Edict of Nantes, fled with his family to Dover in 1686 to join other refugee relations already here. Isaac stayed in Dover and built up a thriving shipping and banking business with offices on land later cleared to extend the Tidal Harbour on its eastern side. At the time of this work Minet moved to an imposing building on Custom House Quay and in 1740 Peter Fector, eighteen or nineteen years old, came from the Low Countries to assist his uncle and, within a few years, took over complete control of the business, greatly extended it and changed its name to Minet & Fector. (Later changed again, this time to Fector & Minet). He became deeply involved in the town's business, administrative and social life and he, or his descendants, acquired large parcels of land in River and Temple Ewell and in some of the land loosely referred to as being in 'Kearsney'.[13]

He married into the Minet family and in 1835 his son, John Minet Fector became the town's Member of Parliament. Connected with that old Dover firm – through the allied interests of the descendants of Isaac's brothers – the name of Minet is preserved in a London financial institution which today mainly provides funds for the provision and extension of airline fleets. How tragic that with the demolition of property to enable the ravages of war to be repaired, and the consequent extension of Russell Street, the name of Fector is lost and that of a small-time property developer is preserved in its place.

In the early 1930s, from the *Castle Inn* at the bottom of Russell Street, Dolphin Lane threaded its way between the Dovor *(sic)* Gas Company, a malthouse and Phœnix Brewery on the left and on the right, Leney's Bottling Store (later, but alas, no more, Martin Walter's workshops), Leney's Cask Yard, Flashman's workshop and Killick & Back, the drapers, to reach the Market Square. Dolphin Lane, named from the dolphins to which ships were moored in the original primitive harbour, is thought by some to be the oldest thoroughfare in the town, being the natural route from the Castle via Hubert Passage, Russell Place and a causeway to the little settlement on the western side of the early harbour. I know of no proof of this theory but it is, at least, plausible. Under some parts of its present tar-mac'd

34 surface there remain the cobble stones used to form a more durable surface when the Paving Commission was, in 1778, given authority to collect stones from the foreshore (if the harbour authorities agreed!) or to use 'good Kentish blue stones' to improve the condition of some of the roads in the town.[1]

The gutter on the east side of Laureston Place is, I believe, the sole remaining piece of visible evidence of the use of these cobbles and I pray this evidence will never be removed as a result of the prevailing pursuit of 'cost effectiveness', or indeed, any other pretext.[14]

Along the line of the boundary between the present day East Kent Garage and the multi-storey car park was Phœnix Lane, connecting Dolphin Lane and St. James's Street. On its NE side was the featureless high brick wall of the Dovor (*sic*) Gas Company but the other side was almost entirely taken up by two of Leney's numerous malt houses. A few yards further on was St. James's Place, with a row of cottages backing on to the brewery on its SW side and running on into St. James's Street. St. James's Lane, a little further on, was, and still is, the road between the river and the frontage of the brewery (now the multi-storey car park) and across St. James's Street to Townwall Street. This lane, from Dolphin Lane to St. James's Street, in some places rather less than four metres wide, was also cobbled and when rainy weather coincided with equinoctial spring tides was flooded at times of high water by the over-flowing river, which was prevented from entering the brewery by walls built from the great piles of sand-bags that were stored in the yard in readiness.

The lower part of St. James's Street (that is from Fector's Place southwest-ward) in the early 30s still showed signs of its earlier importance. Square in the middle of the high wall that surrounded the Gas Company's premises, and forming the SW side of St. James's Street, was the

Lower St. James's Street.
Note the three fire lanes running into Townwall Street

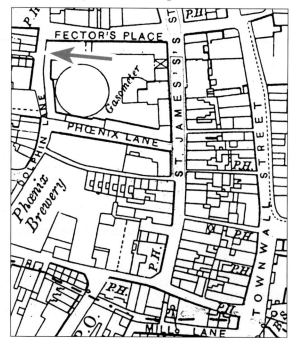

big house of its Managing Engineer, Mr George Dixon (I well remember his two very comely daughters). Almost opposite, a very interesting house, No. 11, was the early home of Peter Hawksfield, founder of the firm of coal merchants that was later taken over by Powell Dufryn and its subsidiary, Corral. By the 1930s the house had been turned into flats. Next door was the Gordon Boys' Orphanage whose founder was the Mr T. Blackman, who was instrumental – with Mr E. Morgan – in forming the Boy Messenger Brigade that operated from Caroline Place. (Mr Blackman was also the treasurer and founder of the Victoria Seaside

Houses at the bottom of St. James's Street in 1930

Orphans' Rest at Hesketh House in Laureston Place). On Sundays the Gordon Boys wore full Scottish dress, but during the week they were rather meanly attired in shorts and a jersey. The boys themselves were entirely responsible for the cleanliness of the home, internally and externally, and for the washing-up necessary after every meal. Those of us who saw them daily gained the impression that their lives were clearly not the happiest.

From the orphanage to St. James's Lane, on the seaward side, the houses were small and many were occupied by traders dealing in second-hand goods or by general shop-keepers. Near the centre of this length of the street were two interesting relics of the days, in the early 17th century,

36 when it was necessary to have fire lanes to separate groups of houses with thatched roofs. One such lane was Townwall Passage, hardly more than a metre wide that opened out into Townwall Street beside the *Sussex A* and the other, no wider, was St. James's Passage, which ran into Townwall Street by the *Granville Hotel* . In St. James's Street between these two passages, but on the other side of the road, at No. 79, was St. Margaret's Place, a cul-de-sac of 9 houses arranged as in a courtyard. Nos. 77 and 79 were large houses of four floors with the front doors adjacent to each other on the first floor, and approached by a flight of 9 or 10 stone steps parallel with the footpath and forming a jagged inverted 'V'. The steps were dangerous as there was no handrail. At the bottom of the inverted 'V' and between the steps was a large block of stone, rather worn, that believe could have originally have had no other purpose than to be used to mount a horse.

At the bottom of the street, on the west corner with St. James's Lane St.was the *Red Lion Inn and Lodging House.* The 1881 census reveals that beside the publican and his staff there were 30 others living there on the day the census was taken. Opposite, that is on the seaward corner of St. James's Street and St. James's Lane, were two of the oldest buildings in the street and by their appearance, with an overhanging first floor, they might well have been in existence at the end of the seventeenth century.

St. James's Lane leading into Townwall Street

James's Lane led on into Townwall Street between the Ice House, operated when I was very young by Mr William Smith, a fishmonger and poulterer whose shop was at the corner of Thornton's Lane, and the *Robin Hood Inn,* which, with other premises north-eastward, was almost totally destroyed by bombs and shells during the 1939-45 war. I particularly remember the Ice House because I was one of the children of the neighbourhood who were often, in summer time, sent there with a large wicker basket and 2d. (less than one penny today) for which sum the basket was filled with broken ice by Mr Smith's apparently always cheerful workmen. The filled baskets then were very heavy, I would hazard a guess that they weighed at least ten kilos. On the way home we would frequently stop to relieve our arms and to suck a lump of ice. As long as the ice lasted we had refreshing cold drinks which our mothers made with lemonade powder and some substance, possibly tartaric acid, which to our delight made the drinks effervesce.

The tiny part of the old Townwall Street that still remains runs from Bench Street to the *Britannia* at the corner with Mill Lane. The shop formerly known as the Bench Street Newsagents, at the corner with Bench Street, was built for Court's, the wine shippers, in or about 1836. Between 1880 and 1905 it was occupied by A. & G. Pipe, milliners and fancy drapers but possibly just prior to 1905, Fletchers, the first chain-store butchers to be established in the town, were installed there and remained there until after World War II. The shop was not, in fact, in Townwall Street but in Bench Street and was numbered 12.[15]

Next door was Wootton's all-embracing grocer's shop, known all over the area for the wide selection that in those days could be bought in its long established grocery and provision store. The next place was Goldfinch's butcher's shop (later moved to the corner of Cherry Tree Avenue and Buckland Avenue). Next to Goldfinch's, at the corner with Thornton's Lane, was Mr Smith's fishmonger's and poulterer's business, where the fish was displayed on sloping marble slabs in the open windows and almost the whole of the front of the premises was hung with the shop's extensive stock of plucked and unplucked poultry — a present-day food inspector's nightmare! It is now Valentino's Restaurant. The same Mr Smith was the owner of the earlier mentioned Ice Store, that stood between the end of Mill and St. James's Lanes, a fish shop in the upper part of Snargate Street and, many years before that, a shop in lower Snargate Street almost opposite the entrance to the Grand Shaft.

On the other side of Thornton's Lane, (a fragment of which may still be seen) was Terson's Auction Rooms which, years before, had housed the printing works of another part of the Terson family, and which, in the 1980s became a gaming machine hall. Next, in my young days, there was a pastry-cook's shop, later rebuilt as Ray Warner's photographic studios (now a car-hire firm's premises) and then, on the corner with Mill Lane was the *Wine Lodge*, later entirely re-built and renamed *The Britannia*.

The Wine Lodge *in the 1930s – it was also a wine importing firm.*

Until the re-making of Townwall Street (the A20) the *Wine Lodge* was very typical of a good class 'pub' in those ports in the south and south-east that also had an annual influx of visitors. The proprietor, Walter Day Adams (another Adams who was not a relation of mine), was well thought-of as an importer of wines and spirits and the twice yearly scene as the barrels and casks, newly arrived from Spain and Portugal, were lined up in Townwall Street from Mill Lane to Bench Street, before being taken to his cellars, was interesting to observe.

Before the building of the National Harbour, Dover was accepted as a well-thought-of watering place and in fact the houses on Marine Parade were built as lodging houses for the numerous visitors. Do not be confused by the term 'lodging houses' – in the last century the words had a connotation very different from today's. The houses provided ample accommodation for wealthy people from London and beyond who would arrive as complete family units with their maid- and man-servants, the nurse-maid for the children, and their brougham for Sir and Madam. Each family would occupy a whole house and stay for a month or more. The town profited by their presence and the bigger shops reflected the affluent life style of their seasonal customers.

Between Mill Lane and St. James's Lane was Smith's ice store with the *Robin Hood* on the corner of St. James's Lane. Beyond the *Robin Hood* was another fishmonger's shop run by the kindly Mrs Spicer and next to her was another pub, *The Chandos* which until the year previously, when the landlord changed, was known as *The Liverpool Arms*. It is unusual to find a simultaneous change of name and occupying publican but when this occurred it often resulted from some misfeasance on the part of the outgoing landlord. A chemist's shop, appropriately owned by Mr Alexander Bottle, a distant relative of mine, was next door and I well remember the red- and green-filled carboys, high up in the window, which seemed then to be the distinguishing mark of a chemist.

North-eastward, in Townwall Street, next to Bottle the Chemist, was, in 1896, a poulterer's and greengrocer's shop run by a Mrs Divers and next to that the *Granville Hotel* – not an hotel in the modern sense, just a pub. At the side of the *Granville Hotel* was one of the original fire lanes, then known as St. James's Passage and on the other side of the lane a Mrs Licence kept a stylish lodging house at No. 35, Barrington House. In 1898 the extensive ground floor of the house was altered to make several business premises, one of which was occupied by the Granville Dairy and another by Emery Bros, Plumbers & Painters. By 1901 the dairy was no more and Mr C. A. Wilde had re-opened the shop as the Granville Cigar Stores. Mr Wilde remained in occupation as a newsagent and tobacconist until 1940 but by the early 1930s Emery Bros had departed to Castle Street and in their place was installed Mr Pittock, a butcher, Mr Fish a green-grocer and a Mr McHardy who ran a Tea Room. With the exception of Mr McHardy all were in occupation until the fateful day in 1940 when the whole area was extensively damaged.

Two houses further on lived a man with the unusual name of Umfreville and next door to him was John Part, a hairdresser. Then came Townwall Passage, another ancient fire lane, and the *Sussex Arms*. One or two smaller properties came next and then the yard and back entrance to the Gordon Boys' Orphanage. Still north-eastwards, within a further ten metres, came Fox Passage, now subsumed into the extended Russell Street, and the *Fox Inn,* marking until the rebuilding after war damage, the end of Townwall Street.

Clarence Street, which could be said to have been a continuation of Townwall Street, was offset to the left by three or four metres and thus the return frontage of No.1 Clarence Street faced directly into Townwall Street. It was occupied by G. J. Buckland & Son who were undertakers and carpenters. We children would

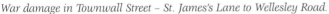

War damage in Townwall Street – St. James's Lane to Wellesley Road.

stand at the wide-open doorway sniffing the smell of oak shavings and watching coffins being made. When we were youngsters Mr Buckland, Snr. would give us offcut sticks with which to propel our wooden hoops and, when we were a little older, the longer sticks we used when playing 'tip-cat'. A five or six inch piece of wood about 1sq inch in section and pointed at each end lay on the ground before us. If we were right-handed we would tap the left-hand pointed bit with Mr Buckland's stick and the 'cat' would leap into the air. One then attempted to smite the falling 'cat' with a mighty whack, the objective being to drive it as far along the road as possible. Unfortunately misdirected contact was inclined to result in a broken window and then we were in deep trouble, from which we could only be extricated by our long-suffering parents who paid for the damage.

The war-damaged central section of Townwall Street – Carter's Grand Garage at R.   *[Roy Chambers]*

The seaward side of the north-east end of Townwall Street was, for about 100m. a rather untidy collection of stores and workshops built on each side of a long bill-poster's hoarding. The hoarding marked the site of an aborted 19th century planned continuation of Russell Street via Liverpool Street and Guilford Lawn to Marine Parade, and, until the 1914-18 war, it con-cealed the undeveloped site on which was later built a Y.M.C.A. recreation room with access from Liverpool Street. The hoarding remained and the Y.M.C.A. continued in occupation until the early days of the last war when the building was converted into a British Restaurant. It was quite severely damaged, almost destroyed, at the time of the bombing of the Grand Hotel, whereon the restaurant moved to St. Mary's Parish Hall in Dieu Stone Lane.

The occupants of the stores and workshops in Townwall Street changed
fairly frequently and could at any one time have been coal and log merchants, car repairers, second-hand clothes dealers, shoe repairers, and indeed any enterprise that needed temporary accommodation. In 1930 the
embryo Ely's Garage was there – remembered well because it was where
I bought my first, (and only), motor-bike, a 350cc Douglas with twin op-
posed cylinders and a maximum speed approaching sixty miles an hour!

A little further westward was, in the early 1900s, the large livery stables
and stores of Easte, (brothers, I think) the corn-chandlers, who were also
in business in Castle Street and farmed at Langdon. My most vivid picture
of the place is of huge shire horses being exercised and the smell of fodder
and hot dung. But when motor cars and motor lorries came into use and
the horse declined as a power source the building was taken over by
Mr R. D. Carter who changed the livery stables into his 'Grand Garage'.
Continuing south-westwards there were two tea rooms separated by a
general shop and a private house, then at the corner of Wellesley Road,
opposite Mr Wilde's shop, was a rather superior second-hand shop that
could very nearly be rated as an antique dealer's establishment.

On the other side of Wellesley Road was No. 8 , 'The Round House',
where, from about 1895 to some time after the end of the First World War
had lived the Revd. T. Shipden Frampton. In about 1933 it housed the
Dover Central Club, a non-political affair and open to all. At this point
Townwall Street was in fact, (and still is), a bridge over the River Dour
although there was no visible evidence to show this. Between 'The Round
House' and Mr Cuff's newsagent's and stationer's shop was a length of tall
brick wall capped by a line of York stone paving slabs. This wall was
simply an upward extension of the bridge's parapet, beyond which the
river ran open to the sky on its course to New Bridge and the Pent. There
was an access door in the wall whence a flight of stone steps led down
to water level which was used by Corporation workmen when cleaning
out the river.

Squeezed between the end of the wall, the river and No. 7 – thus with a
triangular floor-plan – No. 7a was, since about 1915 and until the oubreak
of World War II, the lock-up shop run by Mr T. H. Cuff who had previously
run the stationer's business in what later became the *Hotel de France*.
Though Mr Cuff used it for a much longer period, this particular shop in
Townwall Street, No. 7a, has gone down in history as 'Vickery's Oyster
Shop', a name given to it by troops billetted or operating in the town, even
though its span of use as such was fractional compared with the time it
was a stationer's. After Mr Vickery closed down in 1949 the shop became
a tobaconist's and so remained until its demolition to clear the way for the
formation of the new road to the Eastern Docks.

Nos. 7 and 6 were unusual in that they were built with their backs to the street and their frontages enjoyed an extensive view of the bay which was lost when Camden Crescent was built in 1840. In 1877, when my father came to Dover, he worked for eleven years in No. 6 which was then the premises of Mr R. Hynes, a bookbinder. At No. 5, next door, was the shop and workshops of F. C. Bartholomew, my maternal grandfather. He was a cabinet maker and upholsterer and when my widowed grandmother died in the early 1920s the premises were sold to Hart & Co. who then opened it as a china and glass warehouse, which many will remember.

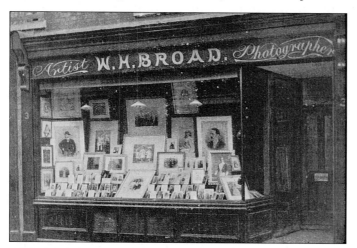

W. H. Broad's shop at 3 Townwall Street

At No. 4 in 1929 was A. W. Pinto, a well-qualified electrical engineer and I remember seeing the very bulky pieces of equipment he stocked, their large size being necessitated by the needs of a 100 volt supply. Dover was one of the earliest towns to have a generating station that was locally owned and locally managed but it was one of the last towns to change over to the CEB's 230 volts. From the last years of the nineteenth century until Townwall Street was no more and was replaced by the A20, No. 3 housed a long succession of photographers, of whom W. H. Broad was the first and Ray Warner the last. Just prior to its demolition Ray moved to a purpose-built shop and studio on the opposite side of the road and many will remember him there, happily at work in his new studio.

The occupiers of No. 3 were, in succession, W. H. Broad, pre-1897 to 1914 or thereabouts, E. V. Bowles to the early 1920s, followed by the notable Miss Dorothy Sherwood until 1938 when she was joined, in the same premises, by Lambert Weston & Sons of Folkestone, with, I know I recall correctly, Ray Warner as manager and subsequently proprietor. Beyond the photographer's shop in 1900 was Farrier & Toms, very fashionable costumiers, whose double-fronted shop was, in 1905, shared with Adams Bros. (no relation), who were cutlers. Just prior to the '14-'18 war it became an equally fashionable hairdresser's and so continued, under changing occupiers, until 1949. No. 1 has, perhaps, a greater claim to fame. From about 1895 until the middle 1920s it housed the dairyman's business of E.W. Farley, later to be amalgamated with A. W.Woodhams, another dairyman, of 41 Castle Street. Mr Farley was Mayor of the town throughout the whole of the 1914-18 war and did not spare himself in caring for the interests of all the townspeople. He was kind and thoughtful and was instrumental in bringing about the lighting, ventilation and extension of many of the caves used as air-raid shelters. At the end of the war he was knighted and became Sir Edwin, the only name that we who were young at the time used for him.

The premises at the junction of Townwall Street and New Bridge had an entrance on the corner, as did the Bench Street News-agent's opposite, and though there was an exten-sive frontage in Townwall Street it was, in fact, No. 1 New Bridge. From a good deal earlier than 1895, probably from the daye of its building, until demoli-tion in 1952 the premises housed an unbroken suc-cession of chemists, the most notable of whom were Harcombe Cuff and Edwin Craig who, between them, covered the period from 1905 until sometime during the last war. By then it had suffered enough bomb damage to make life too un-pleasant for Mr Craig.

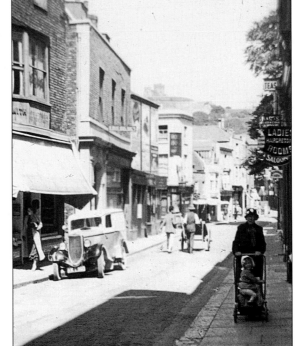

Townwall Street in the early 1930s.

Almost all trace of Town-wall Street disappeared dur-ing the construction of the A20 and the remainder is the group of decaying build-ings at the junction with Bench Street, where the

44 frontages, with the exception of the ground floors, are original and almost untouched. The layby in front of these premises almost exactly defines the width of the old street and the frontages of the buildings on the seaward side of the street were, again almost exactly, where now is the double yellow line on the inshore side of the east-bound carriageway.

Camden Crescent, ten tall and rather distinguished-looking houses extended from New Bridge to the garden of 'The Round House' and until the 1939-'45 war were all, except No. 1, in single occupation. The ground floor of No. 1 housed the very exclusive costumier's and milliner's business of the elitist Misses Todd and Harnden who remained in occupation until the late twenties or early thirties. By that time the other houses in the crescent had been converted into four, and in some cases five, flats and No. 1 soon followed, but by then the Misses Todd & Harnden were replaced by Charles Stewart, a tailor. Nos. 8, 9 and 10 were destroyed by enemy action at the same time that the SW end of Liverpool Street, the *Grand Hotel*, Wellesley Road and 'The Round House' were damaged beyond repair.

In the late forties, in Camden Crescent, No. 1 housed the East Kent Joint Planning Committee, and also the local Fuel Overseer and the offices of the Soldiers' Sailors' and Airmen's Family Association. Later the houses were used as an annexe to the *White Cliffs Hotel* and the *Hotel de France* and later still, as their shipping operations developed, Townsend's took over some of the buildings as their offices and eventually, and until their move to newly built premises in Russell Street, occupied the whole of that part of the crescent not destroyed in 1940.

War damage at Camden Crescent, Wellesley Road, Liverpool Street and the Granville Gardens

Liverpool Street did not make the same deep impression on me as had
the other streets in the Golden Triangle – to my mind it was monochromatic, grey, cold and architecturally monotonous, relieved only by the interesting shape and the off-white mass of the huge *Burlington Hotel*. Woolcomber Street ended at Liverpool Street but the road continued, as Marine Place, to the Sea Front. My mother was born in Marine Place and I had distaff relatives in Liverpool Street, though that did not necessarily endear me to it. Two hundred metres from the Burlington Hotel, Liverpool Street ended in a wide open space, formed by Trevanion Street and, running in from the Sea Front, Douro Place.

Marine Court's SW wall was on Douro Place and on its NE side was the Sea Front Swimming Baths, destroyed by enemy action with great loss of life. Its site, until recently marked by the sunken garden next to Marine Court, is now the site of a new hotel. The garden was sunken because, at the time the site was being restored, there was said to be insufficient rubble and topsoil readily available to fill the huge hole. That may well be so but it did result in a very pretty little garden which Dovorians used until it was decided to fence it in. Next to the Sea Baths was the Dover Rowing Club's boat house, then a store place for a fire-hose reel and a stretcher on a two-wheeled truck, rather like a builder's barrow of the time. In those years the Dover Police (they were Corporation employees then) provided the Fire Brigade and the Ambulance Service. Next was the Territorial Drill Hall, built originally as a skating rink, but in 1915 transformed into a hangar to house a flight of R.N.A.S. seaplanes and some tiny Short Bros.flying boats.

In the last war the hangar's slipway, and indeed, the whole of East Cliff beach as well, was used in the course of training troops in the speedy boarding of landing craft and in assault landings.

Behind the Sea Baths was a long shed in which were stored the Dover Rowing Club's racing craft. Behind Marine Court was a long line of garages, and between the garages and the site of the early gas works, at the far end of Liverpool Street, were some interesting military buildings: the Territorial Field Artillery's Drill Hall, the house where lived the Sgt.Major-Instructor to the Gunners and the Riding School specially built for the training of the mounted members of the Battery. My older half-brother learned to ride there and as Battery Sgt.Major he took the battery to India at the beginning of World War I. At the inshore side of the rowing club's shed was the rectangular cast-iron pissoir, the proposed demolition of which had a mysterious connection with the disappearance of the similar, though circular, structure at the top of St. James's Street.

Soon after the construction of the earlier A20 the Drill Hall and Riding School were demolished and the site was used as a lorry park.

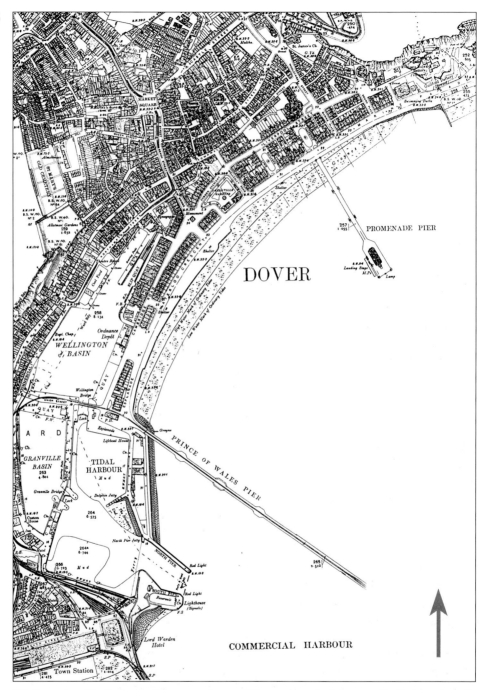

The intentional inclusion in this map of part of the western docks area will allow readers the opportunity to visualise the huge changes made there during the last fifty years.

THE SEA FRONT, MARINE PARADE

THE TWO LAWNS, Guilford and Clarence, laid out between Liverpool Street and Marine Parade, were little more noteworthy than the street itself. They were, however, the sites of two well deserved memorials; in Clarence Lawn was the bust of Capt. Webb who, in 1875, was the first to swim the Channel and in Guilford Lawn there was the statue of The Hon. Charles Rolls, a pioneer aeronautical engineer in the firm of Rolls-Royce, Ltd., who was, in 1905, the first to fly the Channel both ways in a single flight and who died in a crash-landing a few months later.

After major war-damage to the area, fortunately with little harm to the statues beyond some chipping by shrapnel, they were taken away and safely stored, deep underground, in one of the caves so numerous between East Cliff and Fan bay.

After the war Capt. Webb's bust, on its granite plinth, was planted on the north-eastern end of the East Cliff promenade and the statue to Charles Rolls was re-erected near the root of Boundary Groyne, an ideal spot later entirely spoilt by the insensitive construction of a large public convenience within a few metres of the statue. Many Dovorians felt it would be appropriate for both memorials to be re-erected on the Lawns in front of The Gateway where they could be placed near to their original positions.

To clear the way for the extension of the A20 the Webb bust was moved to a spot within a few metres of its original site in the lost Clarence Lawn but the Rolls statue remained *in situ*. Some time later is was disclosed, through a 'leak', that the Department of the Environment, acting through the Ministry of Transport, was about to 'hi-jack' the statue and re-erect it on a site in the area that it had compulsorily acquired for the 'improvement' of the A20. Some members of the Dover Society took up the cudgels and after more than two years of negotiation, the battle was won and as a result of the co-operation of the Society and the Dover Harbour Board the Rolls statue was moved and re-erected on the lawn in front of The Gateway, quite near to its original site in Guilford Lawn. Ownership of the statue is now in the hands of the Dover District Council.

The houses in Marine Parade were not as distinguished as were, and still are, those on Waterloo Crescent, but by and large they served the same purpose, having been built with the primary aim of providing accommodation for visitors with a leavening of local residents. In the centre and also approximately at the centre of the present Gateway flats, was the double-fronted and well-appointed Royal Cinque Ports Yacht Club, with a wide patio and a balcony where, especially before the National Harbour was built, members sat and watched the sailing in the bay.

Until 1939 the promenade, over its whole length, was a scene of great social activity and on Sundays in the summer would be so crowded that it was not possible to walk without weaving to avoid encounters with those walking in the opposite direction. Regatta Day was more than a regatta day and in the evening took on the mantle of carnival. All the essentials for such a celebration were available from stalls and barrows parked in the roadway close up against the promenade railings. They were stocked with balloons and confetti, ice cream and toffee apples, 'teasers' with a feather on the end which unrolled as one blew into them and 'ticklers', more effective, with a bunch of seven or eight brightly coloured feathers stuck into the end of a thin paper tube. We boys used the teasers and ticklers to great effect on all the girls we passed and we had great fun; the day often finished with a firework display on the Prince of Wales Pier.

The Granville Gardens, on the site of the present day garden between the sea and Camden Crescent, were, since the turn of the century and until 1939 the scene of much social activity. From about 1870 onwards military bands performed there, standing on the green. In 1911 a bandstand was erected, followed in the middle 1920s, by a pavilion with glazed walls and a glass roof. In the summer, on Wednesday afternoons, on Saturday evenings and on Sunday afternoons and evenings military bands gave concerts of popular music. Throughout the year there was dancing on Tuesday and Thursday evenings and roller skating on Mondays and Fridays. During the band concerts the young people of the town, of whom I was happily one, would link arms in lines of eight or nine and would march around the gardens, the girls moving, say, clockwise and the boys in the other direction. Or vice versa, I can't remember. Many interesting collisions occurred and many friendships were formed as a result.

There was another bandstand on the promenade opposite Waterloo Crescent where there were performances on Wednesday afternoons, and on that wide open space the bands of the regiments stationed here, or the Buffs (TA), or the Duke of York's School, would Beat Retreat with aplomb and panache not bettered by any Guards regiment and the crowd that watched them just loved it. An 'Entertainments Committee' of the Dover Town Council arranged all the band engagements, organised the firework displays, concerts in the Town Hall and other occasional activities. The committee provided seating for outdoor events and programmes were printed and made freely available to all.

But, as time went on the Dover Corporation was forced, by pressure from the Musicians' Union, to accept the principle that military band engagements, which had been provided for a nominal fee that was considered to be a contribution to the regiment's band fund, could only be entered into at the same rate as would be charged by a professional civilian band. The Corporation realised that at the enhanced rate its budget would not allow it to maintain the frequency of performances to which the townspeople were accustomed and as the frequency declined so did the attendances and the viscous spiral of costs exceeding revenue took its toll until, some little time before the outbreak of World War II, military band engagements were no longer possible and the Corporation was forced to resort to bookings for intermittent performances by amateur bands. It has to be said, however, that the military preoccupation at that time was not with its social commitments but with the grisly problems that lay ahead.

At some point in time (I am not sure of the date) whilst band performances were being restricted for financial reasons, the fun and gaiety of the Sea Front died almost overnight when the parking of mobile stalls and barrows on the road or on the promenade was prohibited.

A typical summer scene on the Sea Front in the 1930s.

I have been reminded more than once that 'The Golden Triangle' is the name of a far-eastern area with sinister connotations. That may well be so, but to me the area in which I grew up and discovered what life was about well merits the name and as the oldest survivor of those born in Castle Street, I am content to use it.

1   To 18th century local Guides, to Bavington Jones in 1907, to Dovorians living on the Sea Front or in its hinterland, to published records of the building of the NationalHarbour and to my peers and me, the jetty near the entrance to the present day Eastern Dock was the "East Cliff Jetty" and the more south-westerly one was the "Castle Jetty". *My East Cliff Jetty* is shewn on Ordnance Survey Maps around 1910-20 as "Castle Jetty" but I am aware that the Ordnance Survey tends to change age old names without any apparent reason and with complete disregard for local usage. I have no idea when the name of *my* Castle Jetty was changed to the less than euphonious "Boundary Groyne" but probably the Harbour Board does, as the jetty itself defines the easternmost extent of the jurisdiction of the Board over the Promenade and the foreshore.

2   Alas my connection with the Castle Street area was snapped when the District Council ordained that our firm should, by the end of March 1990, vacate our premises in Russell Street to facilitate the building of a multi-storey car park on the site and adjacent areas. Demolition began within 24 hours of our leaving. Very soon the area was turned unto a surface car park and the multi-storey idea was "mothballed", so some believe, at the insistence of the Department of the Environment.

3   The estimated population of the separate dwellings is based on the currently accepted assumption that families have 2.4 children. (In this particular case that may well be an under-estimate.) The population of the 52 Burlington Flats is based on assumptions formed from personal knowledge and are that 30% of the accommodation was occupied by single persons, 30% by couples, 30% by couples with 1 child and 10% by couples with 2 children.

4   Mr Offredi made and sold his own toffee which we children of the area valued more highly than "Sharp's Kreemy Toffee" which was the staple of other – to us much less significant – parts of the town.

5   It is difficult to authenticate this parenthetical statement but I have spoken to a few old people who aver that their parents occasionally recalled the usage. There is also some positive pictorial evidence.

6   Much of the information I have on the area of Castle Street is derived from deeds and abstracts that I am very fortunate to possess and which reach back to the early seventeenth century.

7   "Sole" is an old Kentish word for a pond or pool and there are cases where the word was retained when, for various reasons, the water disappeared and the pond became an open space. In 1684 soil was dug from this particular area to be used in the construction of the Long and Cross Walls.

8   The term "The King's Highway' was often used for any road or way not otherwise easily described. I believe it stems from the fact that the land originally belonged to the Crown, as did much of the whole country, and therefore any road or path could be said to be 'the King's Highway".

9   'Folkestone Hill' to Dover Sharks (Dovorians) but 'Dover Hill" to Folkestone Turkeys (Folkestonians).

10   I prefer the name "Castle Place" for the simple reason that in my childhood it was always used. Though it had been "Maison Dieu Road" since the 1860s we used "Eastbrook Place" and "Castle Place" to differentiate those roads from the real Maison Dieu Road, once Charlton Back Lane, which ended at Horsepool Sole. No. 1 Maison Dieu Road is, in fact, on the corner with Dieu Stone Lane, proof positive of where the road was originally considered to begin (or end).

11   12 Castle Street was occupied by J. Webber & Son, Watchmakers and Gunsmiths. The
son was a national rifle shot and was a member of the King's Hundred.

12   The name "Golden Cross" was a reminder of the late 16th and early 17th century gilded cross at a spot approximately where the garden of 46 St James's Street abutted on to the garden of 5 Clarence Street. It was used as an assembly point by itinerant preachers.

13   I discovered the ownership of the lands in River and Temple Ewell on examination of deeds and other documents concerning the land on which Kearsney Bowling Club now stands. As a local government area Kearsney does not exist. The area is within the parishes of River and Temple Ewell and though it is very old it is questionable whether it ever had local government significance. I have traced the name back to 1231 when it was noted as "la Kersun'e" in Fees of Fines and to 1292 when, in the Assize Roll for Kent, it was referred to as "de Kerseneye". Wallenberg says the name is undoubtedly from Old French "cressssonniere' – a place where the cress grows.

14   When the south-western end of the present Dolphin Lane was being 're-vamped' in connection with the building of the multi-storey car park I arranged, on behalf of St. Mary's Old Boys' Association, for two lorry loads of these cobbles to be used to surround a feature in the grounds of the present school, built entirely from materials salvaged from the old school in Queen Street, which houses the bell that was over the gate to the Girls' School in Princes Street.

15   An echo from the past arose when the decrepit Bench Street Newsagent's building was demolished. Workmen clearing up the site discovered in the basement the fascia board that, at some date between 1899 and 1905, was fitted above the Bench Street windows, declaring to all the world, in letters some fifteen inches high, that Messrs A. & G. Pipe, milliners and drapers, were in business there, having just moved the short distance from 182a Snargate Street (next door to W. J. George, the cycle and gun dealer). The building was erected *circa* 1836 and was first occupied by Court's, the wine merchants, who also moved from Snargate Street. Their stores and vaults were on the site of the present day 'Bluebirds' banqueting suite and in the caves behind, under the cliffs.

PART 2

THE EARLY YEARS

1900 – 1918

INTRODUCTION

PART TWO

The Early Years 1900 - 1918

THIS SECTION consists of the recollections of five people, covering the years 1900 to 1918. They are presented mainly as they appeared in *Newsletters*, so they vary in presentation, as some were extracts, some transcribed interviews and some articles.

The first piece is from two interviews with VIOLET CALTON (1895-1994). Violet was interviewed in 1991 and her memories were then transcribed and appeared in two *Newsletters* in the following year, 1992. She lived all her life in Athol Terrace or East Cliff, Dover.

The second contributor, MAY BRADLEY (1905-1995), wrote several short pieces for the *Newsletters* while she was a member. Then, after she died, more of her memories were collected together by the Editor, who was also able to borrow her scrapbook. Many of these pieces were brought together in one article about her childhood which appeared in a *Newsletter* in 1996. For the purposes of this work all her memories have been included in one article based on the original.

Another contribution, which falls in this period, is an extract from a much longer article. In 1989 SIR CLIFFORD JARRETT (1909–1950) wrote reminiscences of his life, which appeared in a *Newsletter* in 1998. The extract chosen for inclusion here refers to his boyhood in Dover in 1917.

HARRY FAGG (1901-1995) was an hereditary freeman of Dover and lived here most of his life. In 1991 he dictated some of his memories to his daughter, Marion Short, a member of the Society, and she sent them for inclusion in the *Newsletter*.

Finally, to conclude this section, are some detailed memories of the childhood of BUDGE ADAMS (born 1909). These were recorded in two 'Interviews with Budge' by Merril Lilley; they were first published in *Newsletters* in 1996 and 1997 and cover the years from 1911 to 1918.

The word pictures evoked in this section of the first two decades of the twentieth century show a Dover few of us would recognise today. Many of them echo names and places already encountered in the 'Golden Triangle' of Part One. The childhood memories of Dover before 1914 make an intriguing contrast with those in Part Three of this book, which depict Dover in the years 1918-1939 and the war memories of 1914-1918 similarly provide a marked contrast with the war memories of 1939-1945 presented in Part Four.

RECOLLECTIONS
of
ATHOL TERRACE and
EAST CLIFF

Violet Calton

The earliest memories of Dover which were collected in the Newsletter were those of Violet Calton, née Gibbs, who lived at No.1 East Cliff. When I met her, in 1991, Violet was 97 years old and almost blind. She was born in 1895. She talked to me and I recorded some of our conversations. I wish I had recorded more of them. She had a sad life, losing her husband in the First World War and her two sons in the Second World War. After that she went to live with her two brothers at No.1 East Cliff and kept house for them. She outlived both of them and was left alone, occupying three floors of the house with a nephew living in the top two floors. When she died her part of the house was left to two granddaughters in America and has, subsequently, been sold. EDITOR.

I WAS BORN 97 YEARS AGO. I've now lived in this house for nearly forty years - the earlier years were spent in Athol Terrace - No. 12. We moved there when my mother had six children. We had to get a bigger house. Our father thought he would buy No. 12 Athol Terrace - in 1895 I think it was - no, 1898 when I was three. We moved in there and then, as the years went on, I had seven more brothers younger than me. It was a very big family but a very nice house. We needed it with such a family, eleven boys and two girls.

My great-grandfather started the horse business. He started in 1842, when he came to Dover. He started horses and cabs. He did very well. He had a wonderful business. He had riding stables. He used to teach ladies to ride. He was a very busy man. He prospered. The stables were down in

56 Flying Horse Lane, just off the Market Square and he had brakes - you know, in the old days instead of going on a bus you'd go on a brake - all open and driven by a couple of horses. Then his son, my grandfather, took it on afterwards, but unfortunately, he only lived to be 42. He had a brain haemorrhage and died so the business went to my mother. She was the eldest of three children and she took on the business from that time and one of the men who worked in the firm fell in love with her and she was married at sixteen.

Possibly one of Violet's father's brakes, waiting at the Monument for pasengers for a 'country drive'.

We used to go to school when we were three in those days and one day when I was coming home from school, from St. James's Street to Athol Terrace, we passed this house, No.1, and it had all the red carpet out and we could see something was happening - and being little girls we were inquisitive- we had to stand and watch - and along came a horse and trap and there was a driver and there was a coachman and he got down and helped the gentleman out - and it was Lord Roberts. He was absolutely one mass of brass, medals, and brass on his hat - and you know in those days they really used to get trimmed up. He came to lunch and the gentleman who lived in this house was General Bruce and he was entertaining him. In those days my father supplied all the horse cabs and that's how we got to know a lot of people. General Bruce was a big customer of my father.   .

I went to St. James's school. It was a little, tiny school but very nice - they were very kind. I believe I am the oldest one alive from St. James's School. St. James's Street was a very busy street. We used to spend our half-pennies in the little sweet shop. It left a great memory. Then Mother thought the school wasn't quite good enough, so she sent me to St. Mary's School. You went to the Market Square and up the hill to St. Mary's School, which was a grade better. You had a place for hanging your clothes and you paid a little each week.

Athol Terrace in 1905 and showing the wall built by S. Pearson & Son

In those days I knew all the people in Athol Terrace and East Cliff. I don't think there's anyone left, not of my age any more. They've all gone.

In No. 4 Athol Terrace there was a titled lady – she used to come down and stay for six weeks in the year and kept that house going all the year. It was next door to my mother's - we lived at No. 3 – Lady Clifford she was. She used to come down and bring her butler and lady's maid and then she had local staff for washing and general work of the house.

The sea used to wash into Athol Terrace, right up to the road and we used to stand there and look down and see the sea and all along Athol Terrace there were wooden stumps and chains in between to stop you from going too near the sea. And I remember my mother always taking my hand, she wouldn't allow me to go out without help in case I fell into the sea. When the harbour came – Sir Whitman Pearson I think it was started to build the harbour – he wanted the ground so somehow or other he forcibly bought it. He gave compensation to each house. My mother had a cheque for £60. In those days it was quite a lot of money. They took all that road away, built it all up and then the next thing we knew we had nothing much left. They left one place, which we called the cutting, where you could sit out and it was quite nice and the children used to play cricket. And then, before we knew where we were, when they were building the docks, they took that piece of ground but they didn't pay anything out and just put a rail around it and took it and that was that.

The prison on the cliffs where now is the National Trust Visitors Centre.

The footpath up the cliffs; that was always there and when I was eight years old I went up there with my brothers. My mother said I wasn't to go, but we'd heard about this man going to fly the channel and it was Bleriot. I heard my brothers getting up in the morning – they were in another bedroom – and I thought 'I'm jolly well going'. So anyway I went with them. The plane had landed and we saw Bleriot in the distance and he stayed in the prison house.

The prison house was on the top of the cliffs and they used to bring the prisoners to Athol Terrace and make them walk up the hill, handcuffed, and there was a policeman with them. They could have gone Castle Hill way but that was a long way round so they made the prisoners walk up the hill and it was very steep (it still is steep!) When the cabs carrying the prisoners came along I used to run indoors because they were big prisoners and you'd see them, chained to the policeman.

Now the whole place is so different. It's so altered. But Athol Terrace
houses are much the same. I think my family owned, at one time, Nos,1,
3, 7, 8, 11, 12, 13, and 14.

I didn't want to leave my house. I liked it up there. We had a lovely
view of the channel, you know, from the drawing room bay window. I
didn't want to leave there but my brothers - one was a bachelor and one
was a widower - they said 'Come for a month'. So I said, 'All right, I'll come
for a month. I can't stay any longer', because I knew what I was in for -
two brothers!! So I stayed for a month and I said, 'I think you'll be alright

East Cliff in the 1920s. Violet Calton lived in the big house on the left of the picture

now'. And they said, 'We can't manage without you. You'll have to stay'.
I said, 'I can't, I really can't', because I didn't want to leave my
house. Anyway, being a sister I suppose I gave way. And that's where I am
now, at No. 1.East Cliff. And when they died they left me the house.

RECOLLECTIONS
of an
EDWARDIAN CHILDHOOD
MAY BRADLEY

ABSTRACTED AND EDITED BY MERRIL LILLEY
from articles and letters written for the Dover Society *Newsletter* and
from the scrapbooks of May Elvey Bradley (1905-1995)

I wonder if the keeping of scrapbooks has gone out of fashion and how many people have such a documented record of their lives as did May Bradley. When she was living in one of the Gateway flats at the end of her life, May wrote to me several times with either articles or letters for the Newsletter and I talked to her about them. After she died I was able to borrow her scrapbooks. From her letters and from the scrapbooks I have compiled this collection of her memories.

I have written only about May Bradley's childhood, ending in 1918, when she went to school in Ipswich. Her story continues in the scrapbook and albums she left, recording the highlights of her life, with photographs, postcards and reports, with notes of her own adding detail to the account.

My thanks to members of May Bradley's family for the loan of her scrapbook and albums and also to Lillian Kay for her invaluable help with this account. *EDITOR.*

MAY WAS BORN, MAY ELVY WILDE, on the 2nd May 1905 at 6.30 a.m. and baptised at St. James's Church on August 30th of the same year. She records that she had a happy, contented childhood and liked to amuse herself.

Her parents, Charles Wilde and Mabel Elvey, were married in St. Mary's Church, Dover on 9th February, 1901. They kept a shop at Barrington House in Townwall Street, selling tobacco, cigarettes and sweets and the family lived in the flat above the shop. Her father had been trained as an electrical engineer in Canterbury, but he chose to start a business in Dover rather than pursue his training. His family were, apparently, upset that he would be branded as a tradesman!

May records that, when she was a child, Townwall Street was a busy place of shops and five public houses! On Friday mornings the 'German band' played in the street near the iron gate leading down to the river, opposite Smith's ice store which stood between Mill and St. James's Lane and straddled the river. Barrington House, No. 35, was a lovely old two-storeyed building with a dozen rooms and a well in the back-yard. The house was directly opposite Wellesley Road and there was a clear view to the sea. The extensive cellars - where later the family sheltered from bombs in the 1914-18 war- were lined with coloured Dutch tiles, some of which may be seen in the Tile section of the Ironbridge Museum.

The shop in Townwall Street where May lived as a child.

On the corner opposite was the Round House, built, so she was told, so that no devils could hide in corners. Across Camden Crescent were the well-loved Granville Gardens and opposite was the Grand Hotel. On the other corner stood a block of red brick buildings and shops, one selling antiques, really 'bric-a-brac', she says, occupied by Mrs.Pritchard and her son Horace, plus a large bad-tempered green and red parrot in his cage outside the shop. The Sailors' Hostel was on the corner of Liverpool Street.

May says that she and her sister, Winifred, had a very happy childhood in a loving home, making the most of their own amusements and going for long walks. They used to walk to the end of Admiralty Pier and watch the building of the new station and landing stages.

Photographs in May's scrapbook show many family groups, many on Dover beach. There is one of May with her sister and a friend in 1909 in their bathing 'drawers' and hats; another one with her mother wearing a green spotted muslin dress opposite the Grand Hotel; another on the zigzag path. Most afternoons were spent on the beach or walking on the hills. May recalls,

'We were great walkers; most winter afternoons, if not at school, one of our parents would take us along the sea front, up the East Cliff path and over the hills behind the castle, returning down the zigzag, probably the old main road up the steep hill, then a pleasant three-laned grassy walk'.

It is the picture of a happy childhood in the years before the first World War.

'A child's life in those peaceful days, of the lower middle class, was happy and protected and , although we did not have much money, our parents were happy and hard working, the shop being open from early morning until eight or later at night and midnight on Christmas Eve'.

There are so many delightful touches about the little things which May remembered from her childhood days, which reveal much about the way of life in the early days of this century and also of Dover during those years. In writing of her childhood, her pursuits, her clothes, her parents and grand-parents, she gives the reader a revealing glimpse of the period one feels privileged to share.

May Bradley, née Wilde, (centre), her sister and a friend.

Her mother's parents moved to Dover and lived in a small house near the docks in Snargate Street, Grandpa giving up his work of repairing and re-decorating large houses and mansions around Canterbury for a tobacconist's shop. Her grandfather, May says, was a kindly man, fond of animals and children and he often made toys for his grandchildren.

'I remember especially a blue painted see-saw, little washing tubs and a doll's house. I still have a miniature chest of drawers full of pens and pencils, which he made over sixty years ago, perfectly finished. It is strange how small things remain in the memory, our pepper black in a grater, but Granny used white in a glass pot and I loved it much better than ours.'

May describes the clothes she wore as a child, many of which she hated; tickly combinations, bodice with buttons, navy serge knickers with cotton linings, flannel petticoat, white petticoat and a dress. She recalled many happy hours spent with her sister on the beach. They wore 'bathing drawers', which were put on over their dresses, plus large straw hats, loaded with flowers. They used the old wooden, horse-drawn bathing boxes in which to change, as they would never have dreamt of undressing on the beach. She says the bathing boxes had a special, exciting smell about them. She remarks, 'How lovely it was to dispense with our many petticoats; the young today do not know how lucky they are to wear so little'.

She also recalls an occasion when her friend Peggy's mother was considered very smart in a black costume with long sleeves and long legs, topped off with a large, frilled, bonnet-shaped rubber cap.

May also has recollections of the sounds of the town; the muffin man's bell when he appeared carrying a large basket of muffins and crumpets on his head; the organ of the hurdy-gurdy man who came every Friday morning with his poor little monkey; the Town Brass Band consisting of three or four blue-uniformed men, playing music under the elm trees by the river and the clamour of noisy rooks which nested in the elm trees.

In summer, she recalls, the military bands played in the Granville Gardens, opposite her parents' shop, morning, afternoon and evening.

The Granville Gardens and the Bandstand where military bands played, principally at weekends

In the interval the bands-men would crowd into the shop and all the family would lend a hand to pour glasses of ginger beer from large stone containers or to press down the glass marbles stopping the bottles of American cream soda, Zola Holm, Cherry Cider and the like. Sometimes, 'much to our delight' says May, the cornet player would ask if he could stand in the front room window on the second floor and play 'echo' solos. The children got to know the bandmasters and bandsmen and could recognise their various uniforms and cap badges.

64   May Bradley wrote a lot about her parents and about the tobacconist and confectionery shop they kept in Snargate Street, wondering how they ever made a living.

'My father must have smoked a good part of thge shop profits, while my mother and sister and I had as many sweets and chocolates as we

May's mother, left, and two of her aunts.

wanted. Many a bar of 1/2d chocolate went down my throat while I looked after the shop while my father went up to have his 'second' dinner. We opened at 8 a.m. and closed at 8 p.m. (9p.m. on Sundays)'.

Almost every year May's parents would arrange a lovely display of be-ribboned chocolate boxes in the large plate glass window, only to have it ruined when the rain seeped through the glass during a gale. May recalls that the shop-soiled sweets were made up into 'Dover bags' and sold cheaply to orphans from a boys' home further up the street.

May started school at the age of six, attending Glenmount School in Godwyne Road. Of her school life May gives details only of her P.T. and dancing lessons.

'P.T. consisted of dumb bells and clubs, swung to martial music, and exercises, at a tumble down hall in the town, when we wore white jerseys and green serge skirts. Music lessons were extra, as was the Saturday morning dancing class, when we were put through our paces by a strict and quick-tempered French woman, but how I loved to charge around in the polka'.

She does record her first 'taste of the literary world', encountering Tiger Tim's comic, Little Folks magazine, a book called 'That Naughty Goblin' and another called 'When the Milkman Came'. Later she progressed to Susie Sunshine of the Rainbow, then the Angela Brazil school stories and Sexton Blake paperbacks.

Amongst out-of-school she mentions cutting girl pictures out of pattern

Picnic at St. Margaret's Bay. May's mother is on the right.

books, sticking them on cardboard and then dressing them up in various frocks and coats by hanging them on the model. May and her sister also enjoyed sticking coloured scraps on a large screen which was put around them at bath time – in a metal hip bath in front of the dining room fire – to shield them from draughts.

Outdoors May and her sister delighted in their first scooters which they rode near their home, charging down a small incline. Also they loved playing in the Granville Gardens, running away from Grandpa and hiding behind some high hedges, much to his annoyance.

In the school holidays they looked forward to the beach and to going for picnics, sometimes as far afield as Folkestone Warren. The family rarely had holidays as summer was the busiest season in the shop. May could remember only a few days in Deal in 1914 and the next holiday after that was a fortnight in Taunton in 1920.

The family had a large, black retriever dog called Jack. Every morning before breakfast, May would take Jack on the sea front and run from one end to the other; she heard later that some people said they could set their watches by her morning run.

So May records the events of her childhood in Dover; the long summers, beach outings and picnics, regattas and band concerts; the winter walks and Christmas Fancy-Dress balls; school routines, music and dancing lessons.

Then, when May was nine years old, the First World War started and gradually her life changed.

In 1915 May's father joined the army and left his wife to look after the shop and the two girls. In May's album is a photograph of a posed family group in 1917, with her father in his uniform. All the other snapshots of this period are of her mother and her two daughters. Father had very little leave. May remembers that on his first leave he gave her a stamp album, which started her on a life-long interest. May tells how her mother, in order to do her bit, gave hospitality to many service men and often had their wives to stay so that they could be with their husbands.

May records that Dover had 185 bombs during the war and she recalls seeing a zeppelin sail majestically over the town.

In 1917 Glenmount School closed down and Miss Moore, the headmistress, went to Ipswich High School and started a boarding house, Broughton House, for the Dover girls. Winifred went to Ipswich in the Spring Term 1918 and May, then aged 13, followed in the Summer Term.

Before going to boarding school May had her hair cut in the new 'bob' fashion, feeling she would be unable to cope with curls on her own.

'Oh, May, What have you done to your hair?' exclaimed the teacher who met her at the station. May felt it was a bad start and says she felt terribly unhappy and homesick. She had never been away from home before. In a way May's childhood ended here, when she went to boarding school in Ipswich at the age of 13.

'It would never have happened but for the war.'

NINE DECADES A DOVORIAN

HARRY FAGG

dictated to his daughter, Marion Short

I WAS BORN IN DOVER IN 1901 at 176 London Road, opposite Buckland Infants' School. I started there at three years old. I remember there was an abbatoir just behind the school, a coal merchant and a coffin maker.

When I was about seven one of my friends and I played hookey and went to look at the abbatoir and when we got there an ox was being slaughtered. I was sick on the spot and ran all the way back to school. In the end I was so ill I was sent home anyway.

When Bleriot landed in 1910 I was eight years old. It was very early in the morning, but when we heard about it we ran up to the castle. We got a good look at the plane even though there were policemen all around it. Afterwards people were charged sixpence a look.

Bleriot's landing in Northfall Meadow in 1909

68　　　The night the first zeppelin came over in 1914 my parents were watching from the window. I woke up when it dropped its bombs near Dover Castle; the casualties were a rabbit and a blackbird.

When the five-masted sailing ship the *Preussen* was wrecked in Fan Bay (now called Langdon Bay) it was mainly loaded with crockery. Our gang and I climbed down the cliffs to get at the china.

The Preussen wrecked and ashore near Langdon Bay

I served with the St. Martin's Scouts at the begining of the war. Bert Brown did duty at the bottom of Whitfield Hill at (Sir) Billie Crundall's house, later taken over by the army. We acted as messenger boys for the military. In 1917 I joined the minesweepers.

One of my uncles, Ben Curtis, worked on the wreck of H.M.S. *Glatton,* sunk in Dover Harbour with much loss of life. It was loaded with explosives and was on fire. The *Glatton* was a ship of the Monitor Class. She was sunk by torpedoes because if she had exploded Dover would have been destroyed. When the order came from Admiral Sir Roger Keyes to sink the ship no warning was given to the 65 men still on board and they were all lost. My uncle was a taciturn man and, on his return from work, was questioned by his wife, my Aunt Flora (my mother's sister) on what it was like down there. Were there many bodies, etc.? His reply was 'Had your tea? Well, I want mine'.

His son Cyril, (who died recently) was also 26 years in the navy and a diver for Dover Harbour Board. He, like me, was an hereditary Freeman of Dover through our mothers, whose maiden name was Williams.

I hardly recognise Dover now. It's all changed so much and so many places have been built over, like Plum Pudding Hill, but I have a lot of exciting memories of it.

An extract from

REMINISCENCES

by

SIR CLIFFORD JARRETT

NOT MANY PEOPLE were bombed out in World War 1, but we were. My father had a photographic business in Dover and when he was called up for the army, early in 1917, my mother managed to carry on the business, with the help of the girl who had been my father's assistant. However, all this suddenly came to an end in the autumn of 1917 when one of the German bombers, which used to make hit-and-run raids on Dover, dropped a bomb in our back garden, which wrecked the studio and made the house uninhabitable. With nowhere else to go, my mother moved to Canterbury to live with her mother and she took my sister with her. I went to live with my father's parents in the Jolly Sailor public house, which my grandfather kept.

As a result of the move to Canterbury, I lost a month's schooling because, at first, the local education authority refused to give me a place because my mother was not a rate payer. Such callous meanness would have been unthinkable in World War II. However, I was eventually admitted to a local elementary school – Payne Smith School, which no longer exists.

I was at this school, which I did not really enjoy, for about a year. Early in 1919 my father was demobilised and his premises were repaired so we were able to resume our old life in Dover. I transferred to St. Mary's School there. (It too has long since been demolished). Life there was rather rugged but it had a superb Deputy Head and the teaching was good, so much so that in 1920 I was able to win a scholarship to the County School – now the Grammar School. There I spent eight happy years and was lucky in being taught by two especially inspiring teachers.

Extracts from some

INTERVIEWS WITH 'BUDGE'

Memories of his childhood and school days

Interviewed and edited by MERRIL LILLEY

MY ONLY CLAIM TO DISTINCTION is that, with a birthday in 1909, I may well be the oldest of the Society's Vice-Presidents, but I have had a very interesting life and by that I mean 'interesting to me'. I certainly remember much that happened to me in my very early years. I suppose, because I was experiencing everything for the first time, the things I saw and did things I saw and did became entries in a great log of memory that has been with me ever since.

STARTING SCHOOL

The memory of my induction into Mr. Ralph's school in Beaconsfield Road is still very clear. I can remember climbing the seven or eight steps to the front door (fearful indeed of what was ahead of me) and being ushered into the room on the right of the entrance where I was set down out of the way of the (to me) enormous children who seemed to fill the room and who sat at desks that were equally enormous. My desk was gigantic! The working surface was at the level of my chin and the very flat angle of my sight line was, I do remember, most uncomfortable. The other children worked with pencils and paper but a clear vignette shows my only equipment was a wooden framed slate, a short length of slate pencil and a piece of damp rag. To the great annoyance of Mr. Ralph (and, I believe, to my great delight) I could make a screeching, irritating sound by holding the pencil flat and rubbing it backwards and forwards across the slate. I can still recall the picture of Mr. Ralph towering above me,

looking at my slate and telling me to 'Get on, boy!' Get on with what?
I most certainly had then, and still have now, no idea. I have the feeling
that this command from Mr. Ralph was fairly frequent.

I remained in the same room, sitting at the same place for a little less
than two years and though it is certain that I did progress from slate and
crayon to paper and pencil I cannot remember, with any clarity, anything
more. However, I must
have learnt something useful, because when, after
Christmas 1914, I was sent
to Barton Road Infants'
School I was not put at the
bottom of the class but near
the top, being accepted as
quite bright and easily able
to read the simple books,
with many pictures and
little text, that were in those
days in plentiful supply.

I feel fairly sure that I
learned to read at home and
at my mother's knee.
I can still picture my
mother and me in the
breakfast room at Millais
Road with, all around us,
piles of wooden blocks,
with different letters on
their six sides. My mother
helped me to form words
and made a game of it.

Mr Ralph's School today, in Beaconsfield Road.

I suspect that, about this time, there began - in the smallest possible way,
not spurred on by my parents - an unplanned but absorbing interest
in philology which, though never profound, has been with me ever since.

It was during my time at Ralph's school that I explored numbers with
my father as my guide. He showed me that five or six or seven horses, or
dogs, or cats, could be denoted by a wiggly sign as well as by a word and
that, therefore, wiggly lines (or figures) were just a code for words, or, in
some cases, complete phrases. Perhaps then began my parallel interest in
Mathematics. I am uncertain about that, but I would like to think it was so.
so. Many years later my parents said they paid 6d a week (quite a large

sum then) to have me at Relf's school and off their hands for a substantial part of the day - apparently they considered the outlay well worthwhile!

WORDS AND PRINTING

My interest in words and printing started in 1915 when the shortage of staff in the printing shop left my father with very little help. This was a year of great significance for me and it is certain that our return to Castle Street in that year set the pattern of my adult life. The shortage of staff resulting from my half-brother Ted and Charles Southey going off to war (they both were in the Territorial Army) and 'Nimble' Burton, the sole compositor being called up for war service early in 1916. was more than critical – it was catastrophic. It left my father almost on his own; only a frail Miss Wells and another young lady whose name `I can no longer recall but who soon left the firm to become a munitions worker, was still with him. In a business such as ours, with its dual base, one man working alone cannot earn enough to support a family. And so I began working in the shop – if what I did can correctly be so described; whether I was pressed into it, persuaded or enticed I cannot remember – I like to think that I went into it of my own volition.

By the end of 1915, at six years old, I was capable of doing Miss Wells's job, feeding the hand-striker pen ruling machine, (we made and produced old-style ledgers and account books) and to do so I stood on a box that was nine or ten inches high. In no sense was this an exploitation of child labour; it was an activity requiring only a moderate degree of manual dexterity and it was something that I wanted to do. I 'worked' in very short snatches, ten or fifteen minutes at a time, and this also suited my ailing father, who was, amongst his numerour jobs, the pen ruler.

As my father became more and more unwell, the work he was able to do became less and less and the business declined until, in 1917, he became seriously ill and he was forced to close down. The workshops below the living quarters then became my playground and so continued until we opened again after Charles Southey's return from the war. My half-brother could see higher horizons and did not return to us.

During my father's illness, my mother was more and more occupied in looking after him and I was left very much to my own devices. I would play with quads and spaces on a 'stone' in the comp. shop, mostly building castles and getting my fingers black with the lead of which the quads were almost entirely made, and the ink – black, of course – that adhered to them. Very soon I was aware of the inter-relationships within the 'American' points system. I questioned why it was called 'American' when it was used in England – later I knew why – and also that diamond, pearl, ruby,

nonpareil and minion, brevier, bourgoise, long- and great-primer, small
pica, pica, double pica and English, were names of type sizes that had
been used since the time of Caxton, and were very difficult to handle.

These obsolescent names and sizes were empirical, with no logical
relationship throughout the size range and though still in use when I was
young (because replacement was costly) they were anachronisms, though
I am sure that I didn't then know either the meaning or use of that word.
It is curious that I still remember all those size names, of which we used
all except the first three, which were almost microscopic.

Although I played in the shop I was not allowed to move or operate any
piece of machinery and my mother kept an eagle eye on me to prevent
me from 'pieing' a case of type. I wondered if my father worried himself
about what I was doing in the shop below. I can't remember doing
anything particularly catastrophic but I was really learning the whys and
wherefores of paper and ink, of type and ruling pens and leather and
glues and all the things covered by the wide diversity of activities in the
workshop of a jobbing printer and bookbinder.

In the early 1920s my father began the replacement of the old type
sizes and, though by the time he became ill not a great deal had been
accomplished, sufficient had been done to whet my appetite for the greater
typographical freedom that the American points system would afford me
and my enthusiasm, as I played with quads and spaces, knew no bounds.
My father, I am sure, realised the value of all this and could see that I was
easily, and entirely subconsciously, absorbing most of the knowledge that
would be necessary to me in the life that was, apparently, already mapped
out for me. When my father could again get about, he taught me to set
type and to find the 'nick' in the letter without looking for it, so that, again
without looking, I could pick up the letter from the type-case put it into in
the composing 'stick', both the right way up and the right way round.
An incidental, but very neccessary, accomplishment for a budding
compositor was to be able to read a page of type from left to right when
the page was upside down, an accomplishment which, in later life, proved
to be valuable on a number of occasions.

The box I used to stand on to feed the ruling machine, nearly two feet
square and about ten inches high, had a hinged lid and was known as the
'Stationery Box' and it contained the shop's entire stock of visiting and
memorial cards in all their sizes and varieties. Later my father bought a
lovely mahogany cupboard with five shelves and panelled doors, salvaged
by the Stanlee Shipbreaking Co. operating in the Camber in what is now
the Eastern Docks, and the name was upgraded to 'Stationery Cupboard'.

With no staff remaining and with my father confined to bed for so long there was, obviously, no income being generated by the business and the family finances reached a critical stage. In those financially dark days my mother, to whom all credit is due, with a sick husband at home and with two very young children, took on an Industrial Insurance book from the Royal Liver Friendly Society and traipsed around the town collecting the weekly premiums. And we survived!

I don't recall doing anything specific to help my mother. My sister did that and I was led to believe that there were other things I should do. I remember that I became quite adept at sharpening a carving knife on a 'steel', and that it was my responsibility to keep all brassware, door knobs and so on, clean and bright. There were, however, two jobs I had to do on a Saturday.

First, I had to scrub the front steps and the basement area at 37 Castle Street and the brick paving outside the back door. I then had to do my grandmother's weekly shopping. She had by this time reached well into her seventies and was almost housebound. The shop she had always used was Faith's, the grocers, at the top of Snargate Street (now an amusement(?) arcade at the seaward end of Bench Street) and in my imagination I can still smell the spices and all the other wonderful things that were

My grandmother's grocer's: Faith's shop, at the top of Snargate Street

stacked all around the shop - mostly in sacks with the tops rolled down like a collar - ready to be scooped up and weighed on a tall, brass beam scale.

At home I received a penny for the work I did and my grandmother gave me another. Combined they were worth less than one of today's pence but that was enough to buy a small bar of 'Sharp's Kreemy Toffee' – made at Maidstone. But before I received my grandmother's penny I had to pay a penance - or so it seemed to me. The old lady (who was, incidentally, an undeviating member of the Plymouth Brethren sect, with all that entails) made a sort of hard, almost rock-like, bun or cake, using, so I was convinced, 95% bicarbonate of soda and 5% flour. Those cakes were vile but I had to eat one before I was given my penny. It was my grandmother's thoughtful, though unsophisticated, way of enhancing my reward, but I could have well done without it.

THE QUEEN STREET ACADEMY

There were no 'catchment area' problems in those days and the high regard in which St. Mary's was held attracted boys from all parts of the town to a school that for many years had been unofficially known as 'The Queen Street Academy'.

6th form St. Mary's School 1924. On left Mr. Wickes, headmaster, on right Mr. Wellden, form master. The writer is sixth boy from the left 3rd row.

My first memory of that school was of standing in front of Mr Wicks, in his headmaster's office, and being asked a wide range of searching questions. After this grilling, for that indeed was what it really was, I heard Mr Wicks say 'Right, Arthur, I will have you in my school'. A Christian name was used only at the conclusion of the headmaster's acceptance interview and the form masters always referred to the boys by their surnames. Mr Wicks went on to say that St. Mary's boys always wore their school caps in public and, on no account, were ever to be seen eating in the street, not even an apple. I was duly installed in Form 3B with Mr Godfrey (an old boy of the school) as form master.

Within a few days of my joining the whole school took part in an 'Air Raid Drill'. Air raid shelters were provided all over the town, mostly in caves in the cliffs and hillsides, but also in street shelters where the population was denser and ad hoc shelters whenever convenient for schools and businesses.

The shelter for St. Mary's was in the basement of Sir Richard Dickeson & Co.'s provision warehouse opposite the school. The Dickeson firm were army canteen contractors dating back to Victorian times and had depôts in all the military towns in the south-east of the country. During the 1914-18 war they were prominent in the N.A.C.B., (the Navy and Army Canteen Board) and later became one of the founder firms of the N.A.A.F.I. In their basement in Queen Street, hung in rows on hooks fixed to long rails slung from the ceiling, were hundreds, perhaps thousands, of sides of bacon. The space between the rows was rather less than a metre and we children sat on the concrete floor in that space. If a bomb had fallen on the building whilst we were sheltering there it would have been difficult, to say the least, to differentiate between the bacon and the boys. Fortunately that problem did not arise.

 We had these 'Take Shelter' practices frequently and the speed we developed in leaving the school building, via a steep staircase, crossing the road, dropping down another flight of stairs into the basement and filing into our places, was little short of miraculous. We knew exactly where we should be in the shelter. We filed out of the classrooms a row at a time, always in the same order, the lower forms going first, and we took up our form's appointed row amongst the sides of bacon. The only time our positions changed was at the beginning of a new school year when most of us had moved up into the next form. This rigid positioning must surely have been designed to assist identification should it ever have been necessary.

I don't think we children saw anything incongruous in all this, but talking in later years to some of the masters, I found them to have been fully aware of the macabre humour of the whole enterprise. Many of us, as I did, whiled away the time by doing 'French knitting', using a cotton reel with five little nails driven in around the hole and operating with a crochet hook. We produced yards and yards of a sort of multi-coloured tubular rope that had no significant use.

AMERICAN TROOPS IN DOVER

All of us were interested to see these men from the New World, especially as they wore Boy Scout hats, riding breeches and putties that very smartly covered their legs - very different from the untidy putties that our troops wore, which very often came undone. Their uniforms were not quite the same shade of khaki and the material was more closely woven and generally better than that provided for the British soldier. But, just as with our own men, their uniforms were often ill-fitting. Where they differed most from our soldiers was not only that they spoke a funny sort of English, spattered with 'heys' and 'says' and referred to children as 'buddies', but also that they seemed to have an enormous store of money at their disposal and were provided with very ample quantities of food to eat.

They were, however, especially to us children living at the foot of Castle Hill, extremely generous. Their ration wagons, long, narrow carts drawn by four mules, moved through Castle Street to Victoria Park, where some of the troops were quartered, and then on to tented camps next to the Naval Air Station on the road to St. Margaret's. The ration wagons were usually piled high with cases, tins, jars, every sort of container and mountains of sacks of potatoes. These things seemed to have been loaded in any old fashion and the stacking was precarious, to say the least. On top of all these items, and even more precariously perched, would be four or five 'doughboys', as I remember they were called. As the wagons moved along the street various items would providentially fall off, always, it seemed where a little knot of children were standing watching. Castle Street was a water-bound macadam road with a high element of chalk in its surface mix. The camber was very high and the tilt it caused must have contributed to the ease with which the items fell from the wagons. The frequency with which seven-pound tins of corned beef fell off kept us busy running off home with our 'findings'. Though there were other desirable items, I remember the corned beef more vividly than anything else.

The American soldiers quartered in Victoria Park were often 'confined to barracks' and would sit on top of the long wall which runs on the left of Castle Hill Road and throw dimes and cents down to us children, who, eager and delighted, scrambled for them.

DE-LOUSING

The de-lousing station on Castle Hill Road was at the left hand corner of the turning off to Canon's Gate where there was a fairly large open space, much like a shallow open bowl. Today the space is filled with nine or ten syca-more trees developed from random seedlings which grew in later years as a result of neglect on the part of the War Office. From 1916 onwards the space was occupied by two corrugated iron covered buildings, from one of which a tall, black chimney belched forth smoke and ashes most of the time. This building was the boiler house and was connected to the other by a number of pipes of varying diameters, all with leaking joints from which most of the steam escaped.

Troops returning from France marched up Castle Hill to the station and undressed 'down to the buff' outside the larger building.Then their clothing, boots, webbing, everything portable, was put into a large sack, which was thrown into the building through an open door. The men were then formed up in fours and were marched, naked as they were, the few yards to enter the other building and the door closed upon them. They were disinfected by, I presume, diluted carbolic acid. I can still smell that carbolic! They then passed into a hot steam chamber and we assumed that on their reappearance they were louse free, but I rather doubt it. One could see them picking over each other in their search for further lice, though perhaps they might have been dead ones   .

Soon after this their clothing was returned to them and they put it on. There was a lot of laughing and ribaldry because much of it had shrunk, especially the underwear and the boots had been subjected to such heat that the leather had lost its suppleness. The soldiers were then marched off to wherever they were to be barracked or billeted.

This was one of the activities in the town that we children hung around to watch. Soldiers were everywhere and none paid attention to us or we to them. We were really part of the total scene.

THE AFTERMATH OF THE ZEEBRUGGE RAID IN 1918

I witnessed the landing of some of the wounded after the Zeebrugge Raid. The casualties were brought ashore at as many places as possible so that they could be attended to without delay and the few that I saw were landed, from smallish boats, on the Promenade Pier (under Admiralty command during World War I). Some were crying out in pain and others lay motionless on stretchers, waiting to be put into ambulances. I stood in the garden of Mr. Fred Kennett, a friend of my father's, on the NE side of the pre-war R.C.P.Y.C. on Marine Parade. In no way could the public have watched the landings of survivors and casualties on the Admiralty Pier, but it was possible to see the damaged ships alongside the pier through the open iron works supporting the shore-ward section of the Prince of Wales Pier and we could see the stretcher cases being brought ashore by huge cranes that lifted them thirty or forty feet into the air.

After the wounded had been dealt with, the other survivors came ashore and later a convoy of lorries took the bodies of those who had been killed to the Market Hall in the Market Square which had been cleared and prepared to act as a mortuary. I can still see the area being hosed down to dispose of the blood and bits and pieces which fell off the stretchers. For many years afterwards it was impossible for me to go near the Hall without sensing again the nauseating stench of violent death.

Later, with a great number of townspeople, I watched the funeral of many of these men. The coffins were put on army lorries, eight on each I think, and covered with Union Jacks. Until then I had never seen a military funeral with a guard party. The guard was drawn up in two lines across the Market Square and along the length of Castle Street. The men stood a yard apart with arms reversed, the muzzle of the rifle resting on the right boot, and the funeral procession, with naval and military escort, passed between the lines, at slow march, on its way, via Maison Dieu Road, to St. James's Cemetery.

THE GLATTON TRAGEDY

H M.M..*Glatton,* fully laden with ammunition and mortar bombs for the British army on the Western Front, caught fire in September 1918 after an on-board explosion as she lay in the harbour at the north-eastern end of the outer line of buoys. She had been moored there to minimise the danger her cargo might present to other naval craft. Much effort was made to rescue the crew. Small ships and little boats went as near as possible to pick them up. I know that fire-fighting and rescue parties from other ships went aboard. One magazine had gone up in the initial explosion and another had been flooded, but the valve to flood the after magazine could not be reached and it was eventually realised that it was not possible to save her. With the considerable store of ammunition still on board, she presented an enormous hazard to other ships in the harbour, to the harbour walls and to the town itself. On the orders of the Senior Naval Officer, Dover, Admiral Sir Roger Keyes, in order to avoid a greater tragedy, she was torpedoed. She quickly capsized and lay in the outer harbour, nearly upside down, for ten or eleven years and was treated locally, if not officially, as a war grave.

I was able to see much of the *Glatton* incident from behind a hedge in the garden of the house at the eastern corner of Marine Parade and Marine Place. I was on the sea front with a friend who lived in St. James's

The Glatton *as she lay in the harbour for many years*

Street, 'Boney' Liddon. (When he grew up he became one of the lifeboat crew). With fixed bayonets (why *fixed* bayonets?, surely there could have been no one they could have used them on) – the soldiers cleared the occupants from the houses on the sea front and townspeople who had gathered there at the sound of the first explosion were cleared off the Parade.

Soldiers who lined the footpath in front of the houses had each a small haversack on his back, wore a steel helmet and had a rifle with bayonet fixed. The men were spaced at about two metre intervals all along the front, with their backs to the sea, and I recall that they noisily 'un-fixed bayonets' before being 'stood at ease'.

The Glatton *as she lay, shunned by all, near the eastern entrance, for almost eleven years.*

'Boney' and I had seen the smoke and flames when the ship caught fire but as everybody was shooed off the sea front we didn't see the torpedoes fired or the resulting explosion. I think it was the noise that drew us back to the sea front, inquisitive to discover what was happening. Perhaps the soldiers were short-sighted, or didn't care, but we crept along close to the houses in Marine Parade, until we reached the garden of the corner house, where we squeezed through a space in the bomb-damaged iron fence and hid in the thick privet hedge, a feature of most fenced gardens in those days. We peered through the hedge, a few metres from the soldiers and saw what we were not intended to see. The badly-burned men were brought ashore on the Promenade Pier, just a little off to our right, south-eastwards. This picture, as with all the Zeebrugge aftermath, will be with me always.

The "Glatton" alongside the west jetty where she lay awaiting the ship-breakers until after World War 2.

In 1939 the *Glatton* was raised and brought in to the Camber where she was laid, partly on her side, alongside the outer side of the West Jetty. A large hole was cut in her bottom and the bodies of those who lost their lives were reclaimed and given a naval funeral. The monitor was later broken up by the Stanlee Shipbreaking Company.

THE MUNICIPAL 'PEACE TREAT'

There was an enormous 'Peace Treat' in Connaught Park in 1919. I remember that the weather was good but most of the details escape me. There was a long slide down the grassy slope from the top path. Whether we slid on mats or a simple sort of sled I am not sure, but the long slide was exhilarating. I remember there was so much to eat it made a great impression on me. There were also street parties where the streets seemed to be decorated with more Union Jacks than there were children. I *know* that there was a Victory Parade in the town because my friends have often spoken of it, but it is not in my memory bank.

PART 3

BETWEEN THE WARS

1918 – 1939

INTRODUCTION

PART THREE

Between the Wars   1918 - 1939

THERE HAVE BEEN so many pieces in various Newsletters about the period between the wars that it has been a difficult task to decide which to include. We have chosen a selection which embrace a wide range of subject matter and viewpoints of people who remember Dover during these years.

The contributions are from members of the Society, with the exception of the first one. This account, by SAMUEL F. ATWOOD, of the Arrival of the Unknown Warrior in Dover in 1920 was written in 1956 and sent to the Editor by his son, David Atwood, who is a member.

The late E.J.BAKER has written of his memories of Dover Harbour between 1915 and 1939 and these cover a variety of topics from 'wonderful events' in the summer regattas to descriptions of the old Marine Station in its heyday.

Many of the memories are of entertainment, of sea bathing, the sea front and the regatta, contributed by DAHLIA HARRIS, JUNE DYER, WINIFRED COPE and A.F.DYER (no relation to June Dyer).

There is another contribution from MAY BRADLEY, a later memory than those in Part Two. Here she describes her time with Dover Guides.

Two pieces describe places, Strond Street by LILLIAN KAY and St. Radigund's Road by JOE HARMAN.

DEREK LEACH has written about a colourful Dover character, Mrs Beresford Baker, having discovered details of her life while he was writing a history of Prospect House.

EDITH MAY KEELER (born 1914) writes of her life in Dover being ;In a Muddle' (Muddle was her maiden name). The recollections in her article range from her very first memories to her marriage in 1938 and continue as far as the year 1945, so the last few paragraphs should rightly flow into Part Four of this book.

In general the period covered here evokes nostalgia, of golden childhood memories, of long summer days and an enjoyment of all the attractions Dover had to offer, especially of the sea front and the harbour. .

THE ARRIVAL
of
THE UNKNOWN WARRIOR
1920
SAMUEL F. ATWOOD

Written in 1956 and sent to the *Newsletter* by his son, David

I T WAS THE OCCASION of the homecoming of the body of the Unknown Warrior when passing through Dover on the journey from the battlefields of France for burial in Westminster Abbey.

As an employee of the Dover Harbour Board, with some colleagues I was enabled to witness the ceremony from the cabin of one of the dockside cranes.

As the destroyer, H.M.S. *Verdun*, bearing the body, approached the quayside we saw the coffin, draped with the Union Jack, on the after part of the ship. Below us on the quayside were representatives of Royalty, the Services, the Church and civic and other dignitaries. Waiting on the quayside was a guard of honour and the band of the Royal Fusiliers, under Bandmaster Bradley.

The vessel safely moored, the pall-bearers proceeded to bring the coffin ashore. As they approached the gangway the band prepared to play, the Bandmaster's baton poised in the air.

What music did we expect? Undoubtedly a funeral march, possibly Chopin's. But, no. As the pall-bearers descended the gangway it was to the stirring music of Elgar's *Land of Hope and Glory.*

Triumphantly the body of the Unknown Warrior was brought ashore to the strains of this martial music. It was a most moving moment, which brought tears to the eyes of onlookers and, now, when I hear the music of *Land of Hope and Glory* I recall this scene with great emotion.

Shortly afterwards I spoke to the bandmaster, expressing my appreciation of the music. He told me that Chopin's Funeral March had been suggested but he thought something more martial was required. He informed his commanding officer accordingly and was told, "Go ahead, Bradley, play *Land of Hope and Glory* if you wish. If everything goes off alright you take the credit, but if there is any adverse criticism, then say it was played under my orders".

ENTERTAINMENT

DAHLIA HARRIS

DOVER IS MY HOME TOWN and was also my husband's. So we always had a great love for it, as many people do. When I was growing up we had a really lovely big theatre here, called The Hippodrome: it was in Snargate Street and it was very well attended, especially when the show was 'Local Talent'.

We also had the Granada Picture House, with its beautiful organ, in Castle Street, the Queen's Hall, the Plaza, and in Buckland, the Regent, later re-named the Odeon. On the Sea Front was the Buff's Drill Hall which held some good dances. In Maison Dieu Road was the Co-op Hall, a really good Social and Dance Hall. On Bunker's Hill there was a jolly good little Scouts' Hut, in which were held dances, socials and beetle drives, jumble sales, etc. – so reasonably priced that my sister and I were quite regular customers there

The Burlington Hotel and Clarence Lawn, from the Sea Front.

and I made lots of friends. There was also the big Burlington Hotel where they had a beautiful Dance Hall, a skating rink, a boxing ring (also used for wrestling and weight-lifting) and people also practised 'keep-fit' there.

At the bandstand on the sea front the local military and marine bands used to play. It was only sixpence to sit in a chair and listen. There were bathing machines on the beach, where people who were shy could change into their bathing costumes.

My sister and I had a very lively childhood.

SEA BATHING

WINIFRED COPE

SWIMMING OFF DOVER BEACH was rather different when I was young than it is now. There was no undresing on the beach between 8 am and 8 pm. We had to use the bathing cabins situated in the Clock Tower area. I felt so grown-up walking on the duck-boards which were laid from the promenade to the sea and intersected the line of cabins. I think the charge was 2d. (two old pence).

Then in all-over swim suits and rubber caps we went into the sea and swam to the raft floating off-shore. Always there was a boatman, rowing up and down and keeping an eye on everybody. I remember so well the rubber roller wringer which we all used to take the water from our swimming suits and the galvanised bath that caught the water.

I am happy that, with so much alteration, our sea front is basically the same.

Bathing boxes (actually tiny cabins to undress - and dress - in). From pre 1880 until the 1920s undressing was not allowed on the beach during normal daylight hours.

DOVER REGATTA
A. F. DYER

WHEN I WAS A YOUNG LAD I used to spend a lot of time on the beach at Dover. I used to talk to the local boatmen and play between the many boats parked up-turned along the beach. I became friendly with Mr Amos, who was a photographer and had a studio in Snargate Street. He owned a whaler and used to take me with some of his friends sailing around the harbour.

I looked forward to the Regatta, as Mr Amos used to enter into the carnival spirit and enter his boat as a 'viking ship". It was always decorated with shields and flags. We used to row along the shore, singing and larking about, to the amusement of the crowds on the beach. Of the crew I can only remember a Mr Sedgewick and his son, who was a signwriter.

To add to the fun, we lads used to buy confetti to put down the necks of girls as they walked along the promenade. They all used to enjoy the happy fun.

In the evening coloured lights were switched on along the promenade and there was always a fireworks display on the Prince of Wales Pier.

Regatta Day. The Promenade Pier made a wonderful grandstand.

STROND STREET
LILLIAN KAY

I LIVED AT 56 STROND STREET, just opposite the heap of coal on to which Hawksfield's unloaded the colliers from Northumberland and Durham and the piles of timber which provided such forbidden joy to the local children. In those days we were allowed 'out to play' after tea. The timber was always piled up with one end absolutely flat; we could clamber up the sides or see-saw on the planks projecting on the far end and, for some reason, our elders thought this was dangerous. The road, of course, was perfectly safe, just a few horses and carts and the very occasional motor car, spotted far away along the Commercial Quay, travelling at about 15 m.p.h. A worse hazard was the engine pulling trucks of coal which appeared out of the Harbour Station, chuffed along Strond Street, round the dock to Union Street, over the swing-bridge to either the Prince of Wales Pier, or right along the Sea Front to the Eastern Arm, all preceded by the man with the red flag. This caused trouble when one was old enough to ride a bicycle, for the wheels slipped neatly into the railway lines.

On Sundays we nearly always had winkles for tea. A boy came round with a basketful which he had collected off the rocks on Saturday and we bought a basketful for a penny. At tea a needle was provided by the plate, to slip off the covering across the opening and winkle out the tasty part. Unfortunately, the really tasty bit is the tail and one has to be quite expert and give a very gentle twist to bring out the whole winkle, otherwise the tail is quite ungettatable.

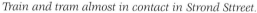

Train and tram almost in contact in Strond Sttreet.

A BIRTHDAY PRESENT

JUNE DYER

I FELL IN LOVE WITH DOVER at the age of six, when I came from Kensington to visit a relative of my mother's who had a commercial boarding house in Castle Street.

The visit made such an impression on me that when the time came for my birthday and my mother asked me what I would like, to her surprise I replied, "I'd like to go to Dover for a week's holiday".

My mother, who had expected me to ask for a party or a present, was taken aback, but, nevertheless, she granted me my wish. She brought my brother and me to Dover for a week.

It was the delight of my life. Dover was so exciting. It must have been Regatta week. I remember being taken at night to the sea front and seeing the lights along the promenade and the moon making a path on the water. From one of the barrows on the front I chose a biff-bat with a little, lurex-covered, paper ball on a piece of elastic. I played with it as I walked along.

June on Dover beach, sitting between her brother and her mother plus her mother's friends visiting from London.

The excitement of the holiday was the beach: it was the nicest beach I had ever known. In my child's eye it became MY beach and MY harbour which should always be kept in order just for me. I remember the Granville Gardens with its deck chairs and bandstand. where the adults used to listen to music, which I found boring. I liked Woolworth's where I spent my 3d pocket money on a little pencil case which looked like a purse and which I carried with me everywhere throughout my holiday. I used to linger in Woolworths, reading books, until my mother pulled me away.

The feeling of excitement which I experienced at the age of six or seven never left me. After the war, to my delight, the family moved to Dover and I have lived here ever since. I never tire of the view from the sea front. When I sit on the verandah of the White Cliffs Hotel (now the Churchill) in the evening and watch the lights come on across the harbour and the path of moonlight on the water, it brings back the memories of my first visit to Dover as a child. The magic has always remained with me.

Mrs BERESFORD BAKER

DEREK LEACH

LITTLE DID I REALISE when I decided to research the history of a building in Dover – the former Prince of Wales Sea Training School – where it would lead me. My starting point was an old photograph of an elderly woman. On the back was written 'Mrs Baker, Founder of the Day Star Mission'. These few words, after much detective work, were to reveal a fascinating story. Isabella Wilson from Knowle in Warwickshire married William Beresford Baker, an Army captain from Ireland, in 1877. By 1890, if not before, they were living at 2 Wellesley Terrace - in one of the four houses that were later converted into the Grand Hotel. The 1891 census shows that they had six servants living in. By 1900 they had moved to 9 Waterloo Crescent.

In 1907 the Bakers bought 11 Princes Street, the adjoining cottages on Durham Hill and the (new) large hall at the rear from Thomas Lewis, a builder. These premises had comprised a private school for young gentlemen, Prospect House, until at least 1905. The adjoining premises, 12 Princes Street (Matlock House) plus the adjacent cottage 1A Cowgate Hill were purchased at the same time from Henry Hutchinson, the school master who had run Prospect House School since 1866.

Mrs Beresford Baker

Dover Directories show Mrs Beresford Baker with a Home of Rest at 11 and 12 Princes Street and her husband, Captain Beresford Baker, living separately at 25 Waterloo Crescent – more about that later! The Day Star Mission Hall on Durham Hill appears for the first time in the 1908 Directory. Then in 1921, Mrs Beresford Baker was still at number 11, Christians' Home Mission, but with Captain William Beresford Baker at number 12, Prospect House. This situation was unchanged until 1934 when Mrs Baker is shown both at the Christians' Home Mission and at Prospect House, her husband having died in 1933.

These are the cold documentary facts but they reveal nothing of the fascinating story that I have discovered from talking to a handful of people who remember Mrs Baker.

Mrs Scott, who was born in 1922 in Bowling Green Terrace and has lived in the locality all her life, told me that the Day Star Mission Hall was run by 'Lady Baker' as she was known locally. She was a very well-to-do regal lady with a superb soft-topped car and chauffeur. Mrs Scott recalls as a young child in the 1920s and 30s everybody in the surrounding (poor) streets would look when Lady Baker ventured out. Mrs Baker was very good to the local people. Every Monday she sent out food parcels to different poor people in the locality. Mrs Scott attended the Day Star Mission Sunday School from the age of four, attending a service in the hall of all age groups which then separated into different classes. At Christmas there

Prospect House circa 1895.

would be a big service and Mrs Baker would sit at a large table covered in brown parcels – the table, not Mrs Baker – with a gift for every child (which was always a garment). The lady missionaries who lived at Mrs Baker's Home of Rest made a lot of the gifts. At Christmas 1930, when Mrs Scott was about eight, she was not given a gift because she had been naughty but was told that she would have it the next week if she behaved – which she did – but the gift was a pair of big bloomers which fitted her mother who was eight months pregnant! The Mission had a Mothers' Meeting on Monday afternoons with a crèche for children but Mrs Scott only went once – her mother was asked to leave her with a neighbour in future! Services for grown ups were held Sunday mornings and evenings.

I managed to find a lady who had given the YMCA – the present owners of the building, – a photograph of Mrs Isabella Baker. The photograph had been given to her by an old friend of 92 who had been her Sunday School teacher at the Mission and who was still alive. I arranged to see her and spent an interesting morning listening to her story. This was Mrs Florence Morris (née Steel) who knew Mrs Baker very well. Her own life story is fascinating; much of it connected with Mrs Beresford Baker and the Day Star Mission. She was born in London but came to live in Dover when she was two. As a small child her mother found out that Mrs Baker's Day Star Mission (as it was known) distributed parcels and gifts to those attending. So Florrie soon attended the Sunday School which was 250 strong and went with her mother to the Monday Mothers' Meeting and the Sunday evening service. Later, Florrie was to be a Sunday School teacher at the Mission for many years. Every Christmas each child would receive two garments made by Mrs Baker's ladies and two oranges handed out by Mrs Baker.

At the age of fourteen Florrie went into service with a Miss Alice Payne, a cripple who lived in Beaconsfield Road and ran a cottage industry with a few girls employed on knitting machines. Florrie did everything for Miss Payne, washing and dressing her, cooking etc. Prayers were always said morning and evening. She also pushed Miss Payne in her wheelchair to the Day Star Mission meetings. As a result Florrie became the 'prodigy' of Mrs Baker with Mrs Baker clothing her, taking her out and taking her for a holiday to her country house at Tenterden.

At 19 years old, Florrie became nanny to the children of Mr and Mrs Cook at Davington Manor, Faversham. Mr Cook was a director of Shepherd Neame, the brewers. After two years Mrs Baker wrote and asked if she would like to go to Africa as nanny to the children of a doctor and his wife who were going as missionaries. Florrie jumped at the chance and returned to Dover; but the good doctor would not take her, insisting that she would be homesick! Florrie returned to Dover and Alice Payne and eventually inherited her business.

Mrs Morris told me that Mrs Baker was a very wealthy woman (presumably the wealth was inherited) who had been presented at court when she was young. Mrs Baker always wore black with white satin fronts. Her clothes and hats were made on the premises. The hats had to allow for her bun to show through. She bought her husband out of the army but 'they never lived together'. He drank a lot and always used a back door to avoid being seen returning from his drinking trips. He lived in one part of the building with his own servants and she in another (Nodd Ffa - House of Repair). She had ten well-to-do retired ladies living with her, known as her ladies-in-waiting. Some of them had been missionaries. They made a lot of clothes for the children of the Sunday School etc. and assisted in the Mission's work. Apparently Mrs Baker also paid for some missionaries abroad.

Mrs Baker had eight maids in uniform – some at least were local girls that had been rescued. Florrie tells the story of going out one day visiting the poor with one of the ladies. At one house they found a fat woman in rags lying on the floor in a completely empty room. They returned to the Mission for food and drink, but Mrs Baker told them to bring the woman back to the Mission. She was given a maid's room, was washed and clothed and became another maid. The maids had to be up at 4am every morning, roused by a retired school governess.

Mrs Baker held 'quiet evenings' for her ladies on Tuesdays. Florrie was invited to attend, but the ladies would not start their discussion saying, 'We are not alone Mother, because Florrie's here'. Mrs Baker replied, 'Florrie is one of us – do I note a spot of jealousy ?' Everybody loved her and she loved them. She was known as our Dover Mother.

Another 90 years old contact, Eric James, told me that she was also known as our Holy Mother. He confirmed that she was well loved and never heard a nasty word said about her. Even so she was strict with her ladies and maids who were never let out of the building without her permission. Tradesmen were often asked to post their letters.

Eric James had a coal merchant's business in Queen Street founded by his father in 1889. He told me that Mrs Baker was a good customer of theirs – particularly at Christmas when she would arrange for the most needy people who attended her Mission to have 3 cwt of coal as well as groceries. He recalls Mrs Baker buying a Ford open tourer car in 1928 but there were few drivers around then. She asked Eric's father for a driver temporarily who would also teach somebody else to drive permanently for her. Eric, who was twenty years old, got the job. He drove Mrs Baker and two of her ladies to (the old) Sainsbury's at Folkestone to shop.

She and two of her ladies would also be driven into the country for picnics – Woolage Green and Nonington, he remembers. Each person, including Eric, was given a packed lunch of good food. She was a stickler for time and punctuality and always told her staff what time she would be back. On one occasion she asked to be driven to Dymchurch but only left three quarters of an hour to be driven back before her scheduled return to Dover. They were ten minutes late and all the staff were waiting outside and gave her a great welcome as if she had been lost !

Eric taught a Mr Hogben to drive the car. He was the husband of one of the maids. On another occasion, when Mr Hogben was able to drive but Eric had to sit alongside to keep an eye on him, an outing to Tenterden was arranged. Mrs Baker hired three single decker open top coaches for the people of the Mission and some of her ladies but she went in the car with two of her ladies and the two drivers. The main party was left to enjoy themselves in a large field near Tenterden but Mrs Baker and her party went off to a big house. The two drivers and a Sister Hilda stayed outside and ate their packed lunches. After lunch Mrs Baker asked to be driven to Heathfield and they all went into a big house. Mrs Baker insisted that they all have a nap before returning, put Eric on a settee, covered him with a blanket and went off herself for her nap which lasted two hours! Then they went back to the big house at Tenterden. Apparently the owner was a missionary - or was it Mrs Baker's Tenterden house ? He proceeded to give a talk about his exploits overseas. Then Eric drove them all home. That was the last time he went out with Mrs Baker because his trainee, Mr Hogben, was considered competent by then – no test in those days. Later Mrs Baker had a row with Mrs Hogben and sacked both her and her husband !

Eric James confirmed that Captain Baker and Mrs Beresford did not live together. Captain Baker had rooms in Prospect House adjoining Cowgate Hill and Mrs Baker occupied Nodd Ffa in the middle and Beresford House at the Durham Hill end. Inside you could move between them all. There was no friction between Mrs Baker and her husband. He was looked after by Mrs Beresford's staff and she saw him occasionally but he was free to do as he pleased. They each had their own interests : Mrs Baker with her Mission work and Captain Baker the Royal Hippodrome in Snargate Street where he was a regular and always had a front row seat - apparently attracted to the chorus girls ! He died in 1933.

Mrs Baker died aged 84 on 23rd October 1938. She was buried in Charlton Cemetery and there I found a distinctive red granite headstone topped by a 12-pointed star – the Day Star.

The headstone is inscribed:

TO THE GLORY OF GOD

AND IN LOVING AND GRATEFUL MEMORY OF

ISABELLA BAKER

FOUNDER OF THE DAY STAR MISSION

WHO ENTERED THE ETERNAL GLORY

23RD OCTOBER 1938

REDEEMED WITH THE PRECIOUS BLOOD OF CHRIST

THY WORD WAS UNTO ME THE

JOY AND REJOICING OF MINE HEART

CAN YOU WONDER WHY IT IS I LOVE HIM SO?

Mrs Morris told me that when Mrs Baker was old she was infatuated with more than one younger man. She used to send her chauffeur for a man who was brought back for breakfast. She tired of him who was then replaced 'by a con man called Captain Geary' (*Mrs Morris's words not mine*). He became a trustee for the properties in 1923 and was one of her executors. According to Mrs Morris, Mrs Baker left virtually everything to Captain Geary on condition that he allowed her ladies to continue living in the house for the rest of their lives. She also left each lady £500 and something for Florrie. However, Captain Geary made life so unbearable for them that they all left and he sold everything. 'He was a rotter!' - according to Mrs Morris.

Captain Geary and his wife then opened the premises as the Day Star Mission Guest House. A small brochure described it as 'a Christian Holiday Home and Guest House, comfortably furnished, gas fires in the bedrooms and bathrooms on each floor with hot and cold water. About 5 minutes walk from the sea and within easy access of station and of buses which run to the beautiful country and places of interest around Dover. Terms from 35/- per week according to room and season. Reductions made for permanent guests. Every care is taken to ensure comfort of guests. Family prayers daily. Services on Sunday and meetings during the week are held in the adjoining Mission Hall'.

Despite Mrs Morris's assertions about Captain Geary it appears that the Mission Hall activities continued for a while after Mrs Baker's death. Eric James told me that Captain Geary was between 40 and 50 when he took over but he did not last a year because he did not have enough money to run the place. Attendances at the Mission dropped off – perhaps because all the perks for the needy stopped.

So ended the era of Mrs Baker and the Day Star Mission but the premises have more to tell with occupation by the WRNS during the war, the opening in 1949 of the Seamen's Residential Club followed in 1953 by the Prince of Wales Sea Training School. After its closure in 1975, Dover College used the premises as a school boarding house for girls until 1994. In 1996 the YMCA purchased the buildings and began renovation work to prepare Prospect House - or Prince of Wales House as it is now called – for the next phase of its extraordinary life.

DOVER GIRL GUIDES

MAY BRADLEY

I was enrolled as a Guide in 1918, at a boarding school in Ipswich, where I was sent during the war. Our Headmistress was our Commissioner and to take our promise we were dressed by our Patrol Leader with a belt, tie, shoulder knots and white haversacks.

After the war I returned to Dover, where the Guide movement was very strong in the twenties and thirties. There were some sixteen companies in the town, plus one in most of the villages. Most were attached to the churches, St. Mary's, St. James's, St. Andrew's, St. Martin's, Wesleyan, Congregational, St. Ursula's, St. Hilda's, Crabble Priory, Holy Trinity and also one at the Duke of York's School. Each year we had District Banner Competitions, plus the annual Guide Play at the Town Hall, which our District Commissioner, Miss Pat Elnor (daughter of the Vicar of St. Mary's) produced in fine style. If ever we met her in the town in mufti, a half-salute was expected. There must be a number of 'Old Guides' who remember her rather autocratic manner, but she was a splendid organiser and we had many happy years in the Guides.

In my 'neck of the woods' at St. James's, we had Brownies, two Guide companies and Sea Guides (later Rangers). We studied astronomy, sea shanties, boat management and swimming and were once invited over to Calais, where we joined a procession to celebrate some event, which I have now forgotten. I remember being very annoyed at not being able to open the windows of our bedroom. It put me off the French for a long time!

At St. James's, on the first Sunday in each month, the whole lot of us, joined by the Cubs and Scouts, marched to church, headed by the pipes and drums of the Gordon Boys, with colours flying – not much traffic in those days!

I remember meeting the Chief Guide, Lady Baden-Powell, over at Hawksdown and getting a last look at Sir Robert, when he disembarked from a cruise liner in the harbour.

SOME MEMORIES
of
DOVER HARBOUR

1915 -1939

E. J. BAKER

MY MOTHER had the sea in her blood. Her father, a ship wright, had a small boat that took a sail and, she told us many a time, at the age of ten or eleven she accompanied her Dad on fishing trips to the east of the Eastern Arm. It was "Lena, you'll be in the boat with me this evening". Sometimes, after missing the tide, it was a case of using the oars until the tide had slackened and they were able to re-enter the harbour.

During gales, after school, my mother used to take us to the Admiralty Pier to witness the wonder and fury of the sea. On New Year's Eve we would be awakened and taken to the garden at Maxton to hear the thrilling sounds of all the ships' hooters and fog horns blasting out a welcome to the New Year. When Royalty arrived at Dover in the royal yacht we would be taken (if after school) to the top of the hill to witness her arrival and to count the twenty-one gun salute.

Regattas were wonderful events. Annually on a summer Wednesday evening, early closing day ,the whole population arose and made its way to the sea front. Trams were loaded to overflowing, pavements thick with walkers, whole families together and the air full of excitement. Sailing races started around noon, doing circuits of the harbour, but from about half past one the delicate racing shells began their events and their flashing coloured blades, depicting their origins, propelled them to and fro across the blue waters. In later years speed boats took part and Bruce Johnston, a nationally-known owner, took part.

Nearer the shore, such events as the "Duck Hunt" took place, where heavy, cumbersome ships' lifeboats, propelled by several rowers, tried to corner a cheeky chappie in a little skiff, while he, dexterously, with oar at the stern, circled in and out of reach, until at last they pelted him with flour bags. On the Promenade Pier, athrong with people, was the 'Greasy Pole' competition. A flag at the end of the pole enticed teams of strong men to compete, but few survived the gap between pier and flag and, as many a competitor, after contortions, lost his balance and crashed into the sea, another would take his place.

On the promenade, barrows parked on the railway lines sold fruit, ice cream, noisy be-ribboned hooters, coloured paper mops, monkeys on elastic, confetti at a penny a bag, and the essential 'ticklers' at tuppence each. Finally, thousands stood still for the fireworks display from the Prince of Wales Pier, "Oohs" and "Aahs" permeating the night air as fantastic colours and images lit the scene. Afterwards began the trek home. Special trams queued for the tired, happy throngs but most walked. What a day! The coloured strings of lights would go out and peace enveloped the scene of such a wonderful family occasion.

An early memory of mine is of the seaplanes, small structures wheeled out from the seaplane sheds, across the road, down the apron and into the water, there to start engines and skim across the water before take-off. This was, maybe, just after the 1914-18 war, for which they had been stationed in Dover.

There was the Feu de Joie on the King's birthday annually, every regiment marching with bands to the Sea Front, the troops strung along the whole length of the promenade from the Clock Tower to the jetty. Then that marvellous sound of the rifles firing continuously, without a break, hundreds and hundreds of staccato explosive, cracking reports, each a birthday greeting, then the cheers of schoolchildren who had been marched down to witness this expression of loyalty.

And all this while, one could tell the state of the tides by sighting the keel of the sunken monitor, H.M.M. *Glatton.* In 1918 this naval vessel, loaded with munitions for the Western Front, had anchored west of the Eastern Entrance. A fire broke out and the duty crew fought the blaze. Men on shore leave were ordered, by megaphone, cinema screen and police notices, to return at once. Alas, the fire could not be controlled and to save the town the Admiral gave the order to torpedo the ship and to sink her. Some 150 men went down with her and she remained there, obstructing the Eastern Entrance, for two decades. Only ships of shallow draught could manoeuvre past her sunken bulk and at low tide her low, grey, whale-like keel could be seen. Eventually just before the 1939-45 war she was brought to the west jetty of the Camber where she was broken up by the Stanlee Shipbreaking Company.

Until the *Glatton* was removed, cross-Channel boats, and for a time, liners, had to use the Western Entrance, doing huge U-turns in order to reverse through the entry to the Admiralty Pier quay side. Unsophisticated stern-only screws failed to get quite alongside, so ropes, leading to thick hawsers, were heaved from deck to shore. Skilful throwing and wondrous catching was needed. The shore force pulled in the hawser, attached it to a bollard and the ship's auxiliary engines pulled the boat sideways to the quay side. As the fenders touched, so the shore force, the porters, came

The Belgian RTM '*PRINSES PAOLA*' *leaving Dover by the Western Entrance in 1972.*

into action. Like monkeys they jumped aboard, scrambled up ropes and moved rapidly round the waiting passengers, even before the ramps had been fixed. Quickly they made deals to move baggage ashore to the Customs and to the boat train. Such hustle and bustle, running and shouting, the object to be first, first to the Customs, first to the boat train, porters hoping for generous tips to supplement their poorly-paid weekly income.

When the train the *Golden Arrow* was instituted groups of children from local schools were allowed aboard the *Canterbury*. My biggest surprise was to see the thick carpeting in all the rooms. We were only used to door mats! However, passengers on the *Golden Arrow* were treated like royalty – and millionaires – and some were!

Once when I was fourteen, to my great joy I was told to go down to Marine Station with the van driver to look after the van and the horses while the driver was delivering. We went to the forecourt by the Lord Warden and parked at the end of the platform between sets of railway lines. Old Mac went off and I held the horse's head. The horse was enormous: I dreaded the advent of a train. But they came and went, snorting, hissing, clattering and smoking and my old horse was quiet as a mouse. Wonderful, especially as he rarely went down to the station. Each train was just a few feet away from us. I was proud of him!

On foggy days a gun was fired intermittently and fog horns blasted mournfully into the grey atmosphere. Every time a gun went off the seagulls left the comfort of cliff ledge, wailing and sighing.

One really delightful sight was that of the red-sailed barges, battling against tide and wind, as they came, through the Eastern Entrance, into the sanctuary of the harbour. They carried grain and had only three crew members; skipper, mate and cabin boy. The herring boats, with tallish smoke stacks, belching out black smoke, came, dipping and leaping, into the haven of Granville Dock, where they discharged their catches to waiting lorries and made ready for sea again. I somehow thought they were the real sailors, their every trip fraught with danger. If you were

lucky a shilling would get you a basket of herrings. But herring have to be followed and after a week or two they were all gone.

I remember in spring, above the packet yard, a beautiful red fox would often lie, sunning herself, or himself, in the warming sunshine. To me the sight of him expressed all the desires of the world that we live peacefully together, Man and Nature.

A sailing barge of the type that traded into Dover.

St. RADIGUND'S ROAD

JOE HARMAN

HAVING LIVED IN THE ROAD all my life I have many memories of it. I think I was about two and a half years old, in 1917, when I recall a big bang and, crawling out from under the bed, where I had been sleeping, seeing my father going out in police uniform. This, I believe, was when a bomb was dropped in Poulton Wood.

The next vivid recollection was in 1922 when one of Nash's horse-drawn carriages arrived to collect my sister and me to take us to the Isolation Hospital with diphtheria. I can still hear the horse, trotting up to Noah's Ark Road and I was not to see my parents for three months.

Five years later I again travelled in one of Nash's carriages to my father's funeral. This could have been one of the last horse-drawn funerals as Mr Nash closed down his stables in 1927.

On November 5th we used to look out to see the local lads queuing up at Guy Mannering's side gate with their guys, hoping for five bob if theirs was approved. I can still see their efforts perched on a four-wheeled truck.One day my truck went out of control and crashed into the gate. I went flying through the air to collect gravel rash on both hands. A little way up the road from our house there was a manhole cover which we used for a game of 'tip cat'. We always kept a weather eye open for the 'Coppers'.

In 1940 one of the first shells landed just above the railway bridge, killing two of our neighbours. Later on in the war, I was walking down the road by Mannering's wall and heard what I thought was a pistol shot and looked around to see the chimney pots spinning off the house opposite. Later I realised that it was the first of another bout of shelling and, luckily, it landed in soft ground in the garden and not too close to the wall.

After the bombing of the East Kent garage, I was working a night shift at the old Buckland tram shed. On coming off duty I felt so rough I made an attempt to see Dr Dick at the Royal Victoria Hospital. I was feeling so ill that I crawled home and went to bed at about 11am. The next thing I remember was that it was 11pm and that I should have been on duty at ten. I had a high temperature and realised that I must report sick.

On going out into the black-out, I put out my hand to open the gate and it was not there – I was sure I was delirious. Next day I was told that work-men had smashed down my fence with sledge-hammers while I was having a good long sleep. I later discovered the trench digging to be the first part of the work of providing electricity for the houses in the area.

After the war I replaced the fence by using old cave-shelter bricks which it was possible to purchase for a reasonable price.

It may surprise some people to know that the road did not get its present name until about 1865, after the railway arrived. Prior to that it was known as Butcher's Lane. A local butcher owned land in the area and there may have been a slaughter-house in the vicinity

I think I can claim to be the longest surviving inhabitant in the road.

Laying electricity cables in St. Radigund's Road in the early 1920s. Prior to this date there was no supply of electricity to this area.

IN A MUDDLE

Edith May Keeler
née Muddle

I WAS BORN IN JUNE 1914 – Mum always said to me, "You were born on 29th June and the war broke out on the 4th August". I was christened Edith May, but to friends and family I was Dinah. It seems the midwife said, "Here's your Dinah", when she gave me to Mum, and so the name stuck. We lived in Manor Road – the Maxton area of Dover. I was the youngest of five, having two brothers and two sisters. We were surrounded by hills so we spent a lot of time on them. Although we didn't have much money we were a happy family.

The tradespeople came around the streets with horses and carts; there were not many motors about then. I remember the milkman came from Hougham, a few miles away. He had a two-wheeled trap and a horse. He had several milk churns on his cart and we took our jugs to buy what milk we needed – it was about one and a half pence a pint (old pence).

I also remember the coalman with lots of bags of coal on his cart. Everybody had coal fires and coal cost about two shillings for a hundredweight. Then, of course, bread and greengrocery were delivered, also groceries and meat. We had several little shops near us which sold nearly everything and we had a post-office.

We had lots of stews, meat puddings and vegetables for dinner, home-made jam and brown sugar on our bread for tea, also home-baked buns.

I don't remember much about the war, only when Dad came home from France when it ended. He was like a stranger to me, but he loved children and we were soon great pals. He had been in the Labour Battalion, digging trenches, as he wasn't fit for the infantry because he had a lame leg. His right ankle had been broken in two places when he was working on the breakwater and the bones would not knit together so they had to be wired. Mum said he was in and out of hospital for a year and they had to postpone their wedding.

I started at Belgrave Infant School when I was five years old. I well remember the big fire in the winter, with a guard around it, and big brown curtains to separate the classrooms. There was a big bell outside the school and the boys took it in turns to pull the rope to bring the children into class.

I was seven years old when I started at St. Martin's Primary School. Miss Preston was my first teacher and I loved her. We had thick sheets of brown paper marked off in inches and pink counters to learn our first sums. I was an average pupil but very shy. My best subjects were composition and drawing. In one of my older classes we had a subject to describe – spring as a young woman. My imagination really ran wild, writing about a beautiful young girl with flowing hair, her feet barely touching the ground and her fingertips changing the bare branches to green. It must have been good for the headmistress read it aloud to the class.

I was in the top class when I left school at fourteen years old. If you were a very bright pupil you could take a scholarship and, if you passed, go on to Dover Grammar School.

Dad was working on the railway. He was a marine dock porter and his wage was about £2 weekly. I remember going to the shop for him, when it was payday, for half-an-ounce of Hearts of Oak tobacco and a packet of A.G. cigarette papers (it was cheaper to roll your own) and I could keep the change, one penny-farthing. What an assortment of sweets you could buy for that amount!

While I was at school I painted a picture in a competition. It was on the children's page in Mum's weekly paper, called *Christian Novels* – it was of two children, sitting in front of the fire and was called 'Faces in the Firelight', so I painted a rosy glow over their faces and clothes and, to my delight, I won ten shillings – First Prize to Edith Muddle of Dover. I remember Mum cutting the results piece out of the book and keeping it until it dropped to pieces.

I had hoped to do something interesting when I began to work, like trimming hats or dressmaking, but I started work as a nursemaid, or mother's help, to the local butcher's wife. They had two little girls, one eight years old and a baby of eight months. It was a busy life.

I learned all the household duties and went out a lot with the baby. I also had the use of an old hand sewing machine and I enjoyed making frocks for the girls and myself. I worked there for seven years. I took the girls to pantomimes at the old Hippodrome in Snargate Street and I went to the cinema every Wednesday when it was my half-day off.

The trams were very handy. They started from the tram sheds which were next to the Orange Tree public house and it cost only 1d to go to Worthington Street. Admission to the cinema was 4d and sweets 2d for a quarter of a pound, so I looked forward to my weekly treat. I was in my teens when the talking films came to the screen. I think 'Laugh, Clown, Laugh' was the first one I saw and I thought it was wonderful.

A tram carrying the bride and her entourage from Belgrave Road to Christ Church.
(The photograph was shot in 1905)

I remember as a teenager going, with some of my friends, to the Market Square to see the old year out. There was a crowd of people already there, all jolly and excited. Then, when the church clock struck midnight, it was so quiet. Then the bells began ringing and we all grabbed hands and danced around, singing Auld Lang Syne; everyone was so friendly and happy, then walking home in the moonlight, shouting to each other "Happy New Year".

We had regatta day in August when the sea front would be full of stalls and people. I think the rowing club had a competition to see who kept afloat the longest, while they pelted each other with flour and soot. My sister and I were walking along one particular regatta day and we met a fellow we knew and his pal, Jim. They walked home with us and that began my friendship with Jim. We were married three years later, in June 1938.

The Second World War began the following year, 3rd September 1939. Jim worked in the tunnel being made in the cliff at East Cliff. It must have been very hard for him as he was a born gardener. He had already registered for war service and was waiting for his age group. When his call-up papers came I think he was glad to get out in the fresh air. He went to Belfast to join his ship, a minelayer called the *Southern Prince*, and he was in the navy for four years.

Dover was called Hell Fire Corner in the war and we had more than our share of bombs. Also when the German troops got as far as the French coast they shelled us frequently and it was the sea that saved us. Many schools and children were evacuated to Wales and, at one time, mothers with young children were advised to have a case packed with clothes and a blanket ready, in case Dover had to be evacuated. Each house had an Ander-

Shakespeare Beach as it was when Edith May was a child.

son shelter in the garden. It was made of corrugated iron and bolted together to form a little room. A big hole was dug in the garden and the shelter erected, then covered with earth. The shelters saved many lives, I packed up many times and took Michael, our young son, to Bexleyheath, where my sister lived, but when the flying bombs, or 'oodle bugs', started coming over on the way to London, I came back to Dover.

The war lasted six years. We had two little sons and longed for a quiet life together. Jim came home on 4th November 1945 and we had a bonfire and fireworks in the garden the next day. We were so happy.   .

Jim started work on the railway as a shunter and we tried to make up for lost time, taking the children out as much as possible. Every fine Sunday in the summer we would go over the hills to Shakespeare Beach. My brother and his wife and family lived next door to us and we made a happy crowd, going up the hill with beach gear, picnic and primus stove.

PART 4

THE SECOND WORLD WAR
1939 –1945

INTRODUCTION

PART FOUR

The Second World War 1939-1945

ALL THE ARTICLES in this section deal with Dover during the war years. The majority of them describe the town during the time of shelling and bombing at the height of the conflict. These include *Wartime Dover* by MAURICE WILSON, *Dover Boyhood Blitz* by GLYN HALE, *September 1940* by JOE HARMAN and the account of the work of Dover's post-office by NAN WHEELER.

Glimpses of events on the sidelines, as it were, are represented by DICK WHITTAMORE'S account of *The Hippodrome, Dover's Frontline Theatre,* NAN WHEELER'S *Extract from a Letter,* FRED FISHER'S *Forgotten Men* and SHIRLEY DOWLE'S *A Sense of Smell.*

DAWN VAUGHAN, returning, with her parents, to live in Dover in 1944, was able to give her view of *The End of the War.*

WARTIME DOVER

© MAURICE WILSON

I WAS BORN IN DOVER in 1927 at a nursing home near the corner of Maison Dieu Road and Taswell Street, and lived in Heathfield Avenue until I was evacuated with the Dover Boys' County School to Ebbw Vale in 1940. Even then I returned home for the school holidays until I left school in 1943, returning to Dover to join my parents (Dad was the Manager of the Maypole Dairy Co. at 48 Biggin Street, next to the King's Hall, a cinema) at their new address in Markland Road.

My first school was Miss Lindsey's, from age five until eight, when I joined Miss Rookwood's class at the County School. In those days it was normal to walk to school if there wasn't a convenient bus route, and my normal route, which it was accepted you did on your own, was down to Barton Path, along to Beaconsfield Road, across the London Road to the raised part (Buckland Terrace) then up past the Chapel to the allotments that ran above Union Road (Coombe Valley Road) and behind the Isolation Hospital in Noah's Ark Road to the top entrance of the school – I believe this walk will be remembered by at least one of our Vice-Presidents! But from the age of ten I graduated to a bike, which was very much easier.

Dover was always a garrison town and we became very used to the Navy and the Army – and each regiment in those days had its own band so there was always an opportunity to listen to them, either playing for the hymns at the Morning Service in the Castle Church or, on any Sunday, on the parade ground at the Grand Shaft Barracks, apart from the special treats, like 'Beating the Retreat' on the Sea Front or marching through the town in ceremonial style on their arrival or departure. That's how I saw my first mounted band and may explain why to this day I am still very fond of brass bands.

Also, there were many, then unexplained, happenings around us at that time – for example, the erection of the massive steel towers behind the Castle. Not until much later did we learn they were for radio-location (Radar).

114 After the war started and the Germans neared the Channel Coast we children quickly learnt about war – in truth, we quite enjoyed it, particularly when the Messerschmitts shot down the barrage balloons that then adorned our town, keeping a score and rushing to pick up the shrapnel, although we soon learnt it would be very hot if we were too quick! Youngsters have no real sense of danger.

One of my most vivid memories of that time was standing on the Admiralty Pier watching all the destroyers and other ships, three or four deep, unloading our troops from Dunkirk to be taken away by train after train. The following week all the local schools joined that railway line as well, and at many stations as we passed through Kent there were volunteers, W.V.S., Mothers' Union etc., waiting to give buns and cups of tea to the weary troops as the trains pulled up to wait for a free line ahead. It must have been a nightmare for the railway authorities to organise, although we didn't think of it as such at the time.

So, after 1941, when I returned home for the holidays, I travelled by bus and always had to show my registration details at the public house outside Swanley, for non-residents were not allowed into the area.

I left Wales for good in 1943, aged sixteen, and first joined the Borough Treasurer's office for about three months until I started in the Westminster Bank. This was in the long building on the corner of the Market Square and King Street, a single storey some sixteen feet wide at the beginning, leading to a two-storey office

The war damaged National Westminster Bank

block above the Manager's Room. This design resulted in a very long underground area, partly a safe where customers' boxes were stored and three other areas for storage, etc.

Normally all staff worked in the banking hall, but during the shelling (to which Dover was subjected from 12th August 1940 until the 26th September 1944) we left the front door open and went down to the main safe where we had set up a counter so that work could still carry on for customers to attend to their business and then wait, if they wished, during long shelling sessions. When this happened, they shared our lunch of sandwiches (the new 'Spam' was very popular) prepared by the ledger keeper. Our typist and adding machine operator shared another cellar, shored up by baulks of timber, while another storage room was occupied outside business hours by fire-watchers, whom I had to join from time to time. Another of my duties at that time was to visit the two upper storeys to check the sand and water buckets, this part of the building being unoccupied and derelict, due to war damage. The bank building was damaged at least sixteen times during the war and it was the bank itself that persevered to

keep a service going. In order to help in this, the main windows, some ten feet high and five feet wide, had been taken out and replaced by a double brick reinforced window high up. The Westminster bank was not the only one to stay open during raids and shelling, for

Buying bread from Chittenden's war damaged bakery in Northampton Street. while Lloyds and

the National Provincial, also in the Market Square, closed, Barclays in Cannon Street and the Midland in Pencester Road, kept open.

It may seem surprising that so many businesses kept going, but there wasn't a lot of choice, for until 1944, at least, shelling and raids were quite sporadic, with sometimes days or even weeks between attacks. And you still had to get home for lunch or after work – all you did was to cycle a little faster through the likely shelling areas! Shells tended to land in Dover in more or less set lines, and it was widely thought that this was because many of the guns were on curving railway tracks and they tended to stop in the same place before firing. This 'straight line of explosions'can be seen by a check of a map published by the *Dover Express* many years ago, and the line I always sped through was the one running from the western side of the Market Square, on behind the post-office, on to De Burgh Street and on further. It is not correct to think that all Dover inhabitants rushed to the caves at every incident – there were many, including all the people I knew, who never saw the inside of any of them!

Altogether 2226 shells, 464 bombs and three parachute mines fell in Dover during the War and in the four years between 1940 and 1944, German guns opened fire, either on convoys in the Straits or on the town itself, sometimes in retaliation to our own guns on top of the cliffs towards St. Margaret's Bay opening fire or, more often, on suspected troop movements or just plain 'bloody-mindedness'. The alert (the normal air raid warning sounded twice) was sounded and the alert continued until usually one hour after the last shell had fallen. Sometimes the Germans fired another soon after the hour was up, and everybody was very annoyed! At the end, however, as our troops (Canadians, I seem to remember) neared the Calais area, shelling became almost continuous, on the last day starting at 2 a.m. with seven in the first hour. More shells were fired in the sea around ten o'clock and at midday the all clear sounded. Before long another shell heralded the beginning of three more hours of continuous bombardment, the very last shell falling on the opposite side of the Market Square (on Hubbard's umbrella shop, where the TSB is now) at quarter past seven in the evening of Tuesday, 26th September 1944. And when it was announced by the Mayor, through the loudspeakers that had been put on lamp posts throughout the main street, that all the gun sites had been captured music was played for the rest of the day. One certain tune – 'Once aboard the lugger, and the girl is mine' – seemed most popular, being played many times throughout the day!

Before then, however, the doodlebug raids had started and while not many fell in Dover, some hitting the cliffs as they came in flying too low to clear, others were shot down by RAF fighters or by the ack-ack guns that had been set up around the coast, some even on our Sea Front. I can still remember being woken one night by a loud harsh vibrating noise and looking through my bedroom window in Markland Road seeing this strange light crossing the sky just above Plum Pudding Hill. When daylight came and we could see these little pilotless planes heading inland we realised what was going on but it was some time before, early one morning, we saw many other planes heading in the opposite direction above the same hill, plane after plane, mostly Dakotas and other planes pulling gliders, on their way, we learned later, for Arnhem and Nijmegen.

DOVER BOYHOOD BLITZ

©S. S. G. HALE

I WAS EIGHT YEARS OF AGE on the 15th August 1940 and my only birthday gift was a wrist watch. The overwound watch was returned within a week to the Biggin Street watchmaker and I was not to see that watch again for many years.

At the beginning of June the WVS made mountains of sandwiches and brewed gallons of tea which were distributed in huge brown teapots by Cubs and Scouts to the carpet of soldiers lying on the Marine Station platforms. Tea was poured into helmets, mess tins, tobacco tins, any container because the Cubs were too small to carry cups and the soldiers seemed to have left everything at Dunkirk. Southern Railway cleared all the soldiers and the following Sunday all the school children too. But there were still plenty of people to watch the skies.

In July the Stuka dive-bombers concentrated on the harbour, but they were vulnerable and even the anti-aircraft gunners managed to down a few and the RAF fighters sorted out the rest. But then the Navy scarpered to Portsmouth leaving only a few MTBs and air-sea rescue launches with Dutch and Norwegian crews which sheltered in the East Cliff submarine pens.

In August a BBC commentator was criticised for reporting the dog-fights in the style of a sports engagement – but that is exactly what it was like. Every downed plane was one of theirs and every victor was one of ours. The after-match scores in 1945 indicated a draw rather than the home win originally claimed. But a Jerry away win was necessary for a successful invasion because the home team still had the Royal Navy in the pavilion at Portsmouth and Scapa Flow. There were playing cards with black silhouettes of friend and foe aircraft and even smaller cigarette cards with coloured pictures to turn everyone into plane recognition experts. If it was diving and had bent wings with its wheels down it was probably a Stuka and if it had two engines it was a Heinkel. At 20,000 feet you could see the contrails, hear the chatter of machine guns, the crump of the anti-aircraft shell explosions (at night the ack-ack shells cracked evilly rather than the day-time crump – something to do with atmospherics).

118 But recognize planes – never! When the Hurricane mistakenly shot down all the barrage balloons along the Folkestone Road it was generally agreed that it was probably a Messerschmitt 109 after all, since it had black crosses all over it. We soon learned to wait for the ack-ack shrapnel, which clattered off the roofs, to cool before adding it to a WWII collection.

The Royal Navy presence was minimal but I suspect the sailors never got past Snargate Street, which provided all the necessary comforts to war-weary seamen. H.M.S. *Lynx,* staffed by WRENs was located at Dover College but wisely moved to the Dover County (now Grammar) School for Boys. The hillside behind the school is still honeycombed with their air-raid shelters. There were lots of RAF and WAAF personnel who ran the radar station at Swingate. There were surprisingly few soldiers who were scattered in penny packets around the perimeter of Dover.

Canadian troops were living in the eight unfinished semi-detached houses at the end of Markland Road. Field kitchens in the gardens provided food. Later the Elms Vale Recreation Ground's changing rooms were the soldiers' dining room. The sloping floor indicated that previously the shed had been a milking shed. The soldiers converted the dairy into a kitchen and dilapidated buildings were repaired and converted into storerooms.The catering staff and service corps personnel remained more or less permanent. The infantry living in civilian homes changed constantly. The GREEN HOWARDS were here. At the end of Bluebell Wood was a company position overlooking the Hougham road. Anti-tank dragon teeth covered by gun positions on both sides of the road were located at the end of the recreation ground (then the municipal dump).

Halfway up Whinless Down behind the Old Barn were two anti-aircraftgun emplacements – but whether there were guns in place depended onwhat army unit was in residence. The concrete and steel girder air-raidshelter behind the Old Barn is still in place. Behind Plum Pudding Hill wasan emergency air strip complete with a tiny brick control tower and camouflaged parking spaces for aircraft. Councillor Law's double garage in Queens Avenue was an AFS fire station but since the firemen were not allowed to use the Law's telephone, communications to HQ were via the Elms Vale public telephone. Occasionally I passed vital messages like "We're running out of sugar" or "When are the spare parts arriving?" But with such communications the station soon closed.

On the 22nd August 1940 everything changed – the first cross-Channel shell arrived. Dover emptied – but fast. The pre-war population was 41,281. The mid-war official guestimate was 14,000. In Bull's description* he suggests 7,000. Another suggested figure for late 1940 was 2,000 which is probably too low but I find it believable. I walked street after street of vacant houses seeing nobody. In Queens Avenue only three families remained, headed by Mr Pelham, power station electrician, Royal Navy Seaman Fidler and coal miner Richard Hale. Everyone with any sense and not vital for defence went. Shops closed, streets were vacated, and schools became rest shelters. The Battle of Britain was almost over – the bombardment of Dover had just begun. I didn't see my watch until 1945 when the watch repairer opened again!

* Bull, Eric "Dover Defences" *ex* Terry Gander, *Military Archaeology.* Stevens 1979.

Hellfire Corner by Brian Petch.

DOVER: SEPTEMBER 1940

JOE HARMAN

W HEN ASKED about my recollections of September 1940 I turned out an old diary and I realised we had been through Dunkirk and that shelling had started: the Battle of Britain was raging around us but no bombs had fallen on the town itself. The barrage balloons had arrived to protect us as fighters were needed elsewhere. German planes came in and shot down the balloons and the crews gallantly put them up again, after disentangling the cables from our chimney-pots.

The real danger was from stray cannon shells and one of the bus drivers had a narrow escape in Barton Road when a shell entered his cab; the scar showed on the dash panel until the vehicle was taken out of service. The bombs, up till then, had been dropped in the harbour or on the surrounding hills, although we did have air-raid alerts because of the battles in the air, and we saw and heard bombers going through to attack the airfields.

On the 4th I noted that I went to the allotment to collect potatoes, carrots and beans. There were no cabbages as the caterpillars had reduced them to bare stalks. We were reliably informed that this was on of Hitler's secret weapons!

On the 7th and the 8th we had bombs on the outskirts. Things began to change on the 9th as there were bombs on Temple Ewell, possibly aimed at the railway

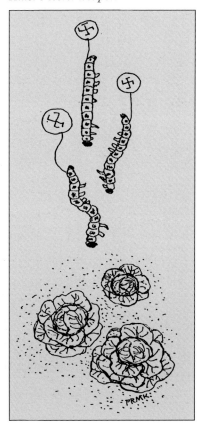

Philomena Kennedey's depiction of Hitler's secret weapon

The Grand Hotel nine years after extensive bomb and shell damage in 1942.

line. Soon after six o'clock we had a bout of shelling, and another at about ten-thirty. The first batch of six appeared to come from separate batteries, judging by their arrival times. I noticed that one included a hit on the Burlington Hotel and I am convinced that the German gunners could see the tower from their side. I now possess a photograph which was taken when a shell struck the building.

The 10th was quiet as I read in my diary that we went to bed from two till eight pm. On the 11th we had a rude awakening but fortunately we had taken cover in our East Kent blast- and splinter-proof shelter when a stick of bombs was dropped, with the last bomb landing a short distance away. When the ground had stopped shaking, and the dust had settled, we emerged to view the devastation.

I grabbed the first aid bag and went along an alley to find the *Sussex Arms* was just a heap of rubble. We then went through into Liverpool Street and found that the *Grand Hotel* had lost a complete wing. I ran up St. James's Street to get help from a first aid post, skirting a bomb crater, and reported the extent of the damage. I was politely told that they were awaiting instructions from Central Control. Some houses opposite the garage were damaged and we concentrated on getting the residents out of cellar shelters. One very large lady was extricated covered in soot and was taken into our shelter. She told us exactly what she would do to Adolph if he ever showed up in Dover. The office girls did their best to clean her up and then produced a welcome cup of tea. I applied sticking plaster in appropriate places. The next day Council staff arrived to demolish the houses by attaching a rope from a lorry to the window frames. This method proved effective as the buildings were old and timber-framed with modern brick fronts. I should have mentioned that shelling started at about the same time on the 11th in the Western Dock area. After 10.30 that night we had bombs in the Folkestone Road area near *The Engineer.*

The 12th was reasonably quiet but on Friday the 13th we had three bombs in the Eßlms Vale area without warning. A bus was standing at the terminus near the recreation ground and the crew had the presence of mind to throw themselves on the floor. Every window was blown out. I remembered bringing this bus back from the paint shop in Thanet the week before. My diary records that I developed a carbuncle on my right arm and I still have the scar to prove it!

On the 15th I was on duty with the Auxiliary Fire Service at the peak of the Battle of Britain and I remember this was the day when most planes were destroyed. I had a week off work because of the carbuncle and at the same time my mother became seriously ill.

It was fairly quiet with various incidents until I returned to work on the 26th when we had shelling in the afternoon, and shells fell again on the 27th. On Monday 30th I went to see our doctor about Mother and he said that she would not last the night through. I came up Ladywell and soon after I reached home we had a bout of shelling which included a direct hit on the Fire Station.

On October 2nd we had bombs in the Clarendon Street area with some casualties but on Friday 4th, the day of the funeral, the only incident was that barrage balloons were brought down in high winds. We felt very exposed as we wended our way up to Charlton Cemetery.

From the postscript to the book

'WAR-TIME DOVER
ITS POST OFFICE AND STAFF'

by A. W. B. MOWBRAY

———

Written by the author's daughter,
NAN WHEELER

THE PERSONAL TRAGEDIES of other people always caused my father real heartache. He had always contacted the telephone exchange to find out where the flashing lights on the switchboard told the operators where there had been any damage in any incident. They could then assess whether the homes of any of the staff might have been damaged. Then he would go out with a driver or union representative to see the position, take some money for immediate needs and offer accommodation. We kept beds aired in our home for those who had lost theirs. Above all, he had a wonderful sense of humour and great faith, which two things kept us all going.

I remember the night of the big air raid on Canterbury – sleep was impossible as the aircraft were overhead. My father came to me around 03.30 and asked if I would catch the 07.00 train to Canterbury as extra staff were needed. So, of course, off I went to find fires still burning and very tired firemen among the snakes of hoses. En route for the Post Office I came to a huge crater stretching right across the road, from one row of damaged houses to another. I climbed down one side and up the other as other people were doing – someone had put boards across. On my return journey in the evening, there was a wire around the crater and a notice saying 'Unexploded Bomb. DANGER' Whoops! My guardian angel had worked overtime.

As Canterbury was a teleprinter centre, there were many circuits linked to places all over the country. Every teleprinter was pouring out tape, needing gumming up on the telegraph forms. The great pile of telegrams waiting to be sent never got less. The engineers drove out to get water for 'gumming up' as we had already drained the radiators and there was no water anywhere. It was some hours before a girl joined me to 'gum up', sticking tape on the telegraph forms ready to be sent out. I glanced at her in greeting and saw that she was black and blue on her face, arms and legs. I asked if she was OK and she said, 'I'm a bit sore, but they've only just dug me out. They dug my Dad out first and he said I should go straight to work, as I'd be needed. They're still digging for my Mum.'

Finishing work one evening in Dover at about 9.00, I was walking out of the back door of the Post Office when Harry Tucker, our dear stalwart of the Home Guard, on duty as usual there, grabbed me and held me against the inner wall just as a diving German aircraft machine-gunned the pavement and the door, tic, tic, tic, and bombs followed. I told Harry I had to go, as I was meeting my father in the Market Square to catch the bus home. Exactly the same thing happened again and this time I was sent to the basement with a flea in my ear. I met my father coming to look for me. We didn't know that the bombs had landed in the Market Square. Good old Home Guard and guardian angel!

Shelling and air raids continued. In one very heavy shelling session which lasted well over thirteen hours, from about 1.00 pm we were stuck in the basement and were beginning to get hungry, especially the early duties. I had been there since 7.00. During a short lull, one engineer ran across the road to his mother's pub and brought back her entire stock of crisps. The Salvation Army members were marvellous and they drove round to all the incidents with their 'char and a wad', regardless of their own very heavy casualty list and were an inspiration to everyone. This time we were OK and they were needed elsewhere.

A voice from our midst suddenly called out, 'Come on, girls. Rally. If we're going to suffer any longer here, we'll fight 'em. Keep up your morale. Out with your powder and show them'. So we all got out our very precious lipsticks and powder. What a cheer went up from the postmen, boy messengers, clerks, chiefs, cleaners, accountants and telegraphists and we all felt much better and able to face up to another seven or eight hours of near misses.

DOVER'S FRONT-LINE THEATRE

DICK WHITTAMORE

FOUR PRIVATE BOXES, 500 seats in the stalls, circle and gallery; five bars (one at each level), a front bar and, entered from Northampton Street, a stage bar; all went to make up the Royal Hippodrome Theatre in Snargate Street, Dover, often affectionately called, in Cockney parlance, the 'Dripping Bone'. Built in 1790 it was one of the oldest theatres in the land and served the folk of Dover for over 150 years before its demise, destroyed by a German long-range shell, in September 1944

A five-piece orchestra accompanied the various variety acts. The leader and first violin was Charlie Haynes who never missed a show although he lived at Kennington, near Ashford and travelled to Dover (which was a restricted area) each evening in an old car for the use of which he received a small petrol ration. Other musicians were Bob Page (piano), Harry Chandler (trumpet), Bill Delahaye (clarinet) and Mr Cooper (second violin). Unfortunately, the theatre drummer left at the outbreak of war and was never officially replaced. The drum kit was still there and another member of the orchestra would lean over and hit a cymbal or give a drum roll when called for. For a while, by kind permission of his Commanding Officer, Jack Rayfield, who in civilian life was Harry Roy's drummer, was allowed to play in the orchestra. Throughout the war the stage manager was Harry Spain. He, too, never missed a show and had been at the theatre for many years.

Secondary lighting at the theatre was by gas, so when the occasion arose that the main lighting failed, usherettes and staff had to stand on chairs, or be lifted up, to light the gas brackets which had no mantles, gave little illumination and were very noisy.

The war-time proprietor, the late H. R. Armstrong, took over the theatre in 1936. Despite all the dangers and difficulties of war, he kept the theatre's flag flying. Very few civilians from Dover's dwindling population visited

The Hippodrome's Snargate Street frontage before it received the attention of the German guns.

the dockside theatre and, therefore, the audiences were made up of members of H.M. Forces, some stationed locally, others just passing through on their way to or returning from the battlefields in Europe. I can also see Mr Armstrong,standing at the front of the blacked-out theatre, informing all that there were "seats in all parts". Also I can see him standing in the front stalls telling the audience that an air-raid or shelling warning had sounded and they could, if they wished, leave and take shelter in one of the many caves in the area. But hardly a soul ever moved. Well, would you have left the theatre knowing that the strip-tease dancer was on next? I wonder!

A very faithful staff of ten dodged bombs and shells and the constant threat of invasion to keep the theatre open. A few names worth mentioning of staff who worked all through up to the fatal day are: George Sidders, the cellarman and senior stage hand, Nobby Granger in the spotlight box and Mrs Hanson, the elderly chief cleaning lady who was a cripple but always managed to get to work from her home in York Street. The usherettes and other staff frequently changed but their services were, nevertheless, greatly appreciated. I make my apologies to any I may have missed.

I started work at the 'Hip' at the age of fourteen in August, 1939, as a page boy. Some may remember my ill-fitting pale blue uniform with lots of buttons and a greasy peaked cap. The first show I saw was a touring version of *The Ovaltinies*. It was a promotion where a disc from a tin of Ovaltine would gain admission. *The Ovaltinies* took up a complete hour and mainly consisted of young budding actors with a finale singing the promotion song, *We are the Ovaltinies* . . . . .

At the outbreak of the war the theatre closed for a few days whilst all windows were blacked out and neon signs disconnected so that no light was visible outside. It re-opened on 12th September with a visit from Robin Richmond with his electric organ in an appropriately named show, *Black Out the Blues*! Variety programmes followed and even two pantomimes were presented that first Christmas of the war. *Babes in the Wood* opened on Christmas Day (Yes, the 'Hip' opened on Christmas Days during the war to entertain the many troops who had nowhere to go), and on 8th January 1940 *Little Bo-Peep* played for six days with matinees. In May Suzette Tarri entertained. It was during that week that a lone Nazi raider dropped one of Dover's first bombs. It landed in the Wellington Dock behind the theatre, in the middle of Henri Hilton's conjuring act — he carried on regardless!

The famous Phyllis Dixey entertained in June and in August the lovely Gloria demonstrated how young ladies of the future would disrobe by electricity! During this time Dunkirk took place, followed by the Battle of Britain with a lot of activity in the skies over Dover.

About this time it was decided to abandon the booking of seats as it was impossible to guarantee performances, so a continuous system was set up – come and go as you please. The summer of 1940 brought the first bombardment from German long-range guns but the Hippodrome carried on. On Monday, 9th September, the 'Hip' had to close through failure of the electricity supply. It re-opened next day, but

The Hippodrome's 'Bill' for 6 Dec., 1943

ROYAL

HIPPODROME

Managing Director—H. R. Armstrong   1943   Telephone 999

5.10 CONTINUOUS PERFORMANCE **7.0**
Week commencing Mon. Dec. 6

The Radio and Film Star

BABS DUDLEY

The Golden Voice and a Piano

RAY and RAYFORD	DeBEAR & DuBRAY
Gay Deceiver & the Nitwit	The Delightful Deceptionists

The Fascinating Nude
:: **GLORIA** ::
In her
Dance of the Seven Veils & Fan Dance

SYD BESSON	THE FIELD SISTERS
Monarch of the Bells Marimba—Xylophonist	Dancers-De-Luxe

JIM NOLAN
A Real Enemy of Gloom

Stalls 3/-, 2/-, 1/6   Circle 2/6   Box Seats 4/-   Pit 1/-
Gallery 8d.

H. G. Wright, Printer, 19b High Street, Dover.

on Wednesday, the 11th, the sea front was badly bombed by hit and run raiders. The Grand Hotel, the Sussex Arms and several properties were hit and casualties were extensive – sixteen killed and twenty-three seriously injured. The theatre escaped damage but there was still no light and the show was abandoned for the week. I well remember, as a page boy, carrying LEON CORTEZ's bag to the station next morning.

After 21st September, 1940, defence regulations were made which restricted cinemas, theatres, clubs and restaurants. They were ordered to close by ten o'clock each evening and they were not permitted to re-open until half-an-hour before sunrise the next day. The local chief of police was also permitted to bring this forward to a nine o'clock closing if he thought this was necessary for public safety. The Hippodrome dutifully changed its houses from 6.30 and 8.50 to 6.00 and 8.00 p.m., and later in the war to 5.10 and 7.00 p.m. During most of the war the last buses used to leave no later than 9 o'clock.

There was no panto at Christmas 1940 but many good variety bills entertained.In April 1941 Sunday ENSA shows first came to Dover. These were arranged by NAAFI at prices of 3d, 6d and 1/-. One ENSA show I particularly remember was *The Ghost Train* which was written by Arnold Ridley (Godfrey of Dad's Army) and he played the rôle of the station master in a tense drama.

The Spring of 1941 brought Dover's 1000th alert and the theatre concentrated on strip shows for the forces. On 15th September 1941, EVELYN LAYE volunteered to play Dover and her £100 salary was donated to local charities. On 15th December TED AND BARBARA ANDREWS starred. They were the parents of JULIE ANDREWS who had a baby with them which I believe was the well-known star of the future.

One week in October 1942 a shell burst in Northampton Street behind the theatre just as it was being cleared. A few slates were cracked, a window was broken and several shrapnel holes appeared in the side of the old building.

During 1942 the Assistant Manager, John Denton, resigned and I was made acting Assistant Manager and full Assistant Manager in January 1943. My duties included ordering the beers, wines and spirits from the brewers (we always over-ordered because supplies were always cut down), looking after the petty cash, keeping the bars supplied with cigarettes and spirits, banking, keeping books and paying the artistes on Saturday night, a practice commonly known in the profession as 'the ghost walking'.

Early in 1943 I had my eighteenth birthday and had to register for National Service. Mr Armstrong tried to get me deferred but it wasn't allowed and I became a BEVIN BOY at Snowdown Colliery in March 1943. I was not too unhappy about this as I was able to live at home and also carry on working at my beloved Hippodrome after my colliery shifts. Also, in common with other civilians, I did one night's fire-watching a week at the theatre, giving our regular night-watchman a night off each Saturday. I have to admit my fire-watching consisted of sitting in the manager's office watching the electric fire all night. I was never called on but was on the premises if anything had happened. A few shells fell in the vicinity on some occasions but I was not disturbed.

One of the greatest shows ever to entertain Dover audiences appeared on Sunday, 19th December, 1943. It came about quite accidentally. A local army unit was to put on a Sunday show in aid of the R.A. Prisoners of War Fund, but the Lord's Day Observance Society intervened and the show had to be cancelled. This was given national press coverage and Tommy Trinder saw it and offered to bring a first class show to Dover that would not infringe any Sunday regulations. The show played to a packed house. Prices: Boxes at 25/- and 20/-, Stalls 4/-, 2/6d and 2/-. Circle 3/-Pit 1/6 and Gallery 1/-. The show, which handed over a nice fat cheque to the Prisoners of War Fund, ran for *three* hours and included TOMMY TRINDER, SONNIE HALE, TESSIE O'SHEA, DEREK ROY, CHERRY LIND, MORETON FRAZER and THE JERRY ALLEN TRIO with their wonderful electric organ. Luckily for us it was a peaceful evening without enemy action.

On 18th January 1944 the last panto ever to play in Dover was *Cinderella*. With two matinees it played to record audiences during a quiet week almost free from the hazards of war. Even some civilians and children visited the old Hip and enjoyed traditional panto.

One night early in 1944 a large stage carpet was stolen from the theatre. Police investigators discovered it cut into pieces and covering the floors in some of the RAF Crash Launches which were moored in the Wellington Dock behind the theatre.

The Hippodrome manager did not prosecute but asked for compensation to the carpet's value. The RAF lads tried stitching the carpet back together but it was no go.

To raise the necessary cash they organised a ball to be held at the Lord Warden Hotel Annexe on Thursday, 17th February, 1944. So *The Carpet Bagger's Ball* took place and the debt was cleared.

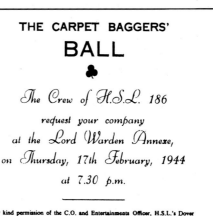

THE CARPET BAGGERS'

BALL

♣

The Crew of H.S.L. 186

request your company

at the Lord Warden Annexe,

on Thursday, 17th February, 1944

at 7.30 p.m.

By kind permission of the C.O. and Entertainments Officer, H.S.L.'s Dover

The organising committee had the nerve to send a complimentary ticket to the Hippodrome Manager! He took it in good part — after all there was a war on!

I can recall a lady in black, who for a time frequented the Hippodrome Bars. It was rumoured she was a spy. Some said she wore a swastika locket and there were others who swore they saw a light shining from her lodging house window at night. She never said much, but was she listening? However, one night she didn't show up and we never saw her again! I wonder?

The badly damaged Royal Hippodrome *and adjacent buildings, looking up Snargate Street towards New Bridge*

"BEAUTY'S IN TOWN" attracted good houses during the weeks of 10th April and again on 21st August. In all this revue played Dover four times during 1943 and 1944.

In the week of 28th August three performances of a variety bill were interrupted by shellfire, and during the week of 11th September only two-and-a half performances were possible. At this time the Canadian Forces were marching up the French coast and capturing the long-range guns. The German gunners continued to bombard Dover by day and night in an attempt to get rid of their shells before capitulation. The bill that week (the last ever to play the Hip) included Renara (renowned pianist), Joe Peterson (the singing choir-boy), Frank E. West (comedian), Rex Ashley, Sonia, Billy

Barr and Lady, and the Six Dancing Diamonds. After the misfortune of that week it was decided to close the theatre for a week and re-open on Monday, 25th September when it was hoped that the threat of shelling would be over. A variety bill was booked and SANDY POWELL offered to appear on the Wednesday as a guest star. Alas, it was not to be. The theatre never re-opened. On Monday 25th September 1944, at approximately midday, Hitler dealt his final blow and the Hip was very badly damaged by one of the final shells from the long-range guns. This was all the more unfortunate because the very last shell to land in Dover left the Nazi gun on Tuesday, 26th September. It hit an umbrella shop just off the Market Square. The Hip was beaten by twenty-four hours! After the theatre was so badly damaged, first-aid repairs were made, and the front street bar was re-opened. It so remained until 1950.

The *Kent Messenger* in 1950, mourning the old theatre as it was being demolished to make way for dock extensions and road widening, said "A former patron, Mr L. Mason, told a *Messenger* reporter, "The bar under the stage had such a unique atmosphere that the finest war artistes of Britain and America, try as they did, could not get it down on paper. It defied English tradition and allowed artistes to come in wearing stage make-up and costumes to have a drink with civilians and servicemen from the audience".

I would like to conclude by recalling one or two interesting items about the Hip. The telephone number was, believe it or not, DOVER 999. Yes, it's true – if you wanted the police in those days you rang Dover 100!

Whilst the theatre never closed, during the early part of the war, in 1944, when things got really hectic, the powers that be enforced closure during shelling warnings.

Very often phone calls were received to ask members of certain MGB's and MTB's to return to their boats. To avoid fake calls, at the beginning of each day's programme, the officer of the day would ring and identify himself, then when we had a call we asked for identification. On two occasions we received a message that *ALL* servicemen were to return to their bases. This nearly emptied the theatre and the 'turns' played to half-a-dozen or so civilians.

One evening, during the last interval, an usherette was stabbed in the 'gods'. An ex boy-friend ran up the gallery steps, stabbed the girl, then ran out and gave himself up near the clock tower on the sea front. The show continued whilst the usherette received treatment and awaited the ambulance. She wasn't badly hurt and returned to work within a few weeks.

On several occasions, unbeknown to the public, the show opened on

Monday night with only two or three acts. However, others arrived, made a quick change, dashed up on to the stage and ensured continuity. This sort of thing happened when Dover was in the news after shelling attacks and artistes were very reluctant to play the nearest theatre to the enemy, and doctors' notes arrived cancelling contracts. The theatre's agent, the Universal Variety Agency, of Haymarket, always managed to find substitutes.

Theatre digs. There were several in Dover where the acts stayed. Locations were in Chapel Place, the Shakespeare Chambers, the Esplanade, London Road and others. Some top-of-the-bill acts stayed at the Half-Way House on the Canterbury Road, and others returned each night to their homes in London.

Variety artistes were very poorly paid, especially when one takes into account the weeks when they were resting. A top-of-the-bill would earn £25 to £30, whilst supporting acts managed any sum from £10 to £20. Out of this they paid 10% to their booking agent, their digs, their travelling between theatres, their make-up and costume costs and 'tips' and gratuities.

This is my story of Dover's Royal Hippodrome during those frightful war days, but, despite everything, they were some of the best days of my life and remain very clear in my memory to this day.

Recently, you may know, a plaque to the Hippodrome's memory has been installed on the wall of the Dover Gateway Hovertel, opposite the site where the theatre once proudly stood.

There is also a seat in the Granville Gardens commemorating the wartime proprietor, the well-known H. R. Armstrong, and on my death I have arranged for another seat, in my name, to be placed somewhere in Snargate Street, thus ensuring three focal points which will, I hope, remind future generations of Dovorians, and others, of the important part played by the Royal Hippodrome Theatre in the life of the town from 1790 to 1944.

EXTRACTS FROM A LETTER
written in 1942

———

NAN WHEELER

During the 1939-45 War the English Speaking Union of America bought, furnished and equipped a cottage in Barham for the use of all the Girls' Clubs in Dover, Deal and Folkestone, to enable their members to have a short break from shelling, bombing and other horrors of war. Nan Wheeler visited the cottage, called 'White Cliffs', with parties of Girl Guides and Sea Rangers.

In 1942 she was asked to write a letter on behalf of the Girl Guide Association to the American people responsible for funding this project. The following are extracts from her letter. EDITOR

SOME OF US are Air Raid Wardens, some Fire Brigade workers, some First Aid party, as well as our daytime jobs, and to know that we need not scramble out of bed, drag on slacks and sweater, snatch a tin hat and rush to our post for goodness knows how long, or how many times a night, is just 'paradise'.

Sunday morning sees Edith waking us with cups of tea. In a short time we are ready for church where we arrive for 8.0 am Holy Communion. The villagers are very friendly and speak to us as we make our way home to a breakfast of bacon, tomatoes, fried bread *and* eggs (!) which Evelyn's mother kindly sent from their home. Some of us had almost forgotten what they looked like. ... We ... climb the hills to a wood. In a clearing there we have a very beautiful ceremony at which Phoebe and Nan are enrolled as Rangers. Around us we find wild strawberries and modest wood violets, quite three months out of season. ... With our spread we have some cider. Our first drink is a toast "To our friends in America". In the afternoon we walk to a nearby farm where a Ranger friend of ours lives. It is called "Heart's Delight" and is a perfect Kentish farm, living up to its name. There are oast-houses, where the hops from neighbouring hop-fields are roasted, and stretching away up the hillsides are the orchards ... Tea over, we wend our way round the village, then return 'home' to ...pack up the goods, and say "bye-bye" till next time. Oh! how we wish we were there for at least a week!

... that visit will always stand as a landmark in our passage through the war. It gave us much relief from strain. Although after thousands of alerts one ignores them, yet there is always the subconscious thought that there is nothing to prevent a shell just where you are, or hurling death from the skies on those you love so much. Our eyes had become accustomed to noticing a flash over the Channel: we started counting, and when eighty had been reached we dodged into shelter – or carried on – or else knew nothing at all. Our ears have become accustomed to the burr, burr, burr of bombers' engines, the pop-pop-pop of machine guns, and the swish of a bomb, and we know that it is tin-hat time. Now, however, we see more of your Air Force or ours, or together, about. We listen to ascertain whether they have gone just to the French coast when we shall hear rumbles and our windows and doors will rattle as the Germans and their accomplices

WHITE CLIFFS, the cottage at Barham.

suffer for their pig-headedness. Every one of our party has known the horror of finding homes and precious belongings gone, or our places of work mauled about, or worst of all, the absence of workmates to whom we were talking only the day before and with whom never again will be shared the joys and hardships of our work. Then it is we pause and wonder, where does all this lead to, and why should innocent people suffer? But a feeling of revenge, mingled with profound sympathy for those who may not even think about the whys and wherefores of it all, spurs us on to renewed efforts. We know that those who gave their lives would say it was worthwhile, and even little children must suffer, as a lead towards that glorious end when all people shall be free.

Accounts of blitzes, raids, etc. may be read in books, so perhaps a few amusing stories of incidents in raids here will be more unusual.

A fellow some of us work with is very disabled and can only walk with the aid of a crutch. He had just left hospital after treatment, when a plane dived, releasing its bombs across the town. Our friend lay flat in the gutter and was quite unhurt. He tried to get up but had difficulty owing to his infirmity. An ardent First Aid Party member rushed up and ordered him to lay still. His protests were overruled and a whistle brought an ambulance, which, in a few seconds, whisked the gentleman to the hospital he had left only a few minutes before, but this time, as he walked away, he left a gaping F.A.P. member and a smiling nurse.

A sneak raider dropped a bomb which sent shoppers hurrying into doorways. When they crept out the road was covered with pamphlets. Hurrah! a leaflet raid! Everyone swooped for a trophy, only to discover they were blown from a nearby shop.

A gentleman sold fish from a barrow outside the Museum in our Market Square. When an aircraft dive-bombed overhead he popped under his barrow – not much protection! When he emerged, his eyes widened as he saw on his barrow in place of fish, two stuffed ducks blown from the Museum!

Phoebe ran to the Fire Station to report for duty when the alarm sounded. She rang the bell outside for admittance, and alarmed the whole neighbourhood as a fire engine came rushing out and enquired from our frightened friend where the fire was? She didn't know she had sounded the main alarm in error.

FORGOTTEN MEN?

FRED FISHER

W ATER IS, PERHAPS, the most important of Man's requirements, on a par with breathable air. Water is the life-blood of the world. Most people know that, but take it for granted; until *they* are *without it.* Unlike other commodities, water is the only thing we *can not do without.* There is no alternative. It is of even greater importance during times of war.

I would like to describe to you the work carried out during the 1939-45 conflict by a small group of nine men who, during the whole of that period, had the difficult job of maintaining the supply of water to the town of Dover, regardless of prevailing conditions.

The, then, Dover Corporation Water Supply Department was the body responsible for the repair and maintenance of Council houses, water mains and services, and fire hydrants within the Dover Town area.

At the outbreak of the war, it had a total of nine men working in the department, with its workshop situated on the corner of Stembrook at the junction with Caroline Place.

In 1941, at the age of fourteen, I managed to obtain a rather menial job working for the Dover Corporation in the town baths, looking after the boiler and general '.dogsbody'. My wage (sic) was twelve shillings and sixpence for a 48 hour week. Fortunately, that job didn't last long because the bathhouse was totally destroyed by a long-range shell. I was then transferred to the Water Supply Dept. and had the privilege of working with these men for the remaining four years of the war.

Much has been said about the work carried out by such people as rescue workers, fire services, police, wardens, and so on, and one must admire those people for the sterling work they did but, virtually nothing was mentioned about electricity, gas, sewage, and water workers. There was no romance to that type of work, yet these people were on call twenty- four hours each and every day, particularly gas and water workers. At night there was a rota system whereby three men from the water department were stationed at the A.R.P. post in Lewisham Road (post war, Buckland Creameries) in order to carry out any emergency action outside normal working hours. I do not propose to describe everything they had to do, but simply give a few examples.

In the event of buildings or roads suffering bomb or shell damage, water gushing everywhere would invariably be a major factor and would require immediate attention, regardless of continuing enemy action. When aircraft were about, then one could, perhaps, have time to take some kind of shelter. It was a completely different situation where shelling was the case. Hardly a day passed, particularly during the years 1942 to 1944, when we could not be found working in a hole full of water repairing a main, or trying to stop the flow of water from a wrecked building. Some of the mains had to be replaced time and time again because of damage from subsequent attacks. Trevanion Street, St. James' Street, and Priory Road, to name a few, spring to mind. On a number of occasions we were faced with a hole half filled with water and a sea of flame owing to a cracked gas main. The flames were usually extinguished by applying wet mud to the cracks if they could be located but, sometimes, the source of the gas leak could not be seen, the gas having seeped through the earth. These were very 'hairy' times. Having to enter a recently damaged building to control the flow of water was, also, a risky business.

At one point in time several of us had to travel to Canterbury to assist with the repair of broken mains, after that city was bombed.

The lower area of the town, docks and sea front were 'no go' areas, and special passes were issued to residents and workmen who needed access. Barriers were erected across some of the main streets leading to those areas. I still have possession of my passes. One particularly onerous job was having to carry out repairs to the water fittings inside the caves and other underground shelters. Some of the people virtually lived in them and the stench was appalling. We called them 'troglodytes'. Such is the price of fear.

Our workshop was destroyed by a shell and we had to relocate to the basement of the Peter Street Hall. It was necessary for us then to use some of the cells in the old police station under the Town Hall in order to put some of the smaller stores. We also used a partly wrecked house in Hawksbury Street to store some of the larger pieces of pipe work. Apart from being blown over by blast on three occasions, none of us received any injury.

As the Canadians were advancing on the German gun sites, shelling became much more intense and I remember working in a hole behind the *'Prince Albert'* pub in Priory Road when it was announced the gun sites had been captured and there would be no more shelling. After that, things became a lot easier for everyone. At the conclusion of hostilities the town was honoured by the presence of the King and Queen. We, together with the town dignitaries, and others who had worked during the war period, were presented to them in Dover Town Hall.

For the record, may I mention the names of my wartime colleagues, all of whom are now sadly deceased? Stan Ross, Joe Fleeman, Albert Dolbear, Frank Smith, Arthur Taylor, Bert Hadden, Fred Andrews, 'Skipper' Alexander and Alf Cook.

A SENSE OF SMELL

SHIRLEY DOWLE

AMONG THE DREADFUL, FRIGHTENING MEMORIES of the war I have two totally different memories – two very aromatic smells. I can almost hear some of you saying, 'How can that be during a time of hard food rationing?' Let me enlighten you.

My Dad, Mr. Frank Abbott, had a small-holding, with about 40 pigs, 100 chickens, rabbits, a horse, etc. In the cookhouse, dominating half the space, was a huge copper, fuelled by a fire underneath. Twice a day – morning and evening – this copper would be half filled with water. Into this was thrown buckets and buckets of 'SWILL'. This swill was people's left-over food, potato peelings, cabbage leaves, apple cores, etc. Householders had to keep these in a separate container from the ordinary rubbish. After about one to two hours all this would be bubbling away and shovelsful of bran would be added to thicken it. By this time the smell was like that of a massive stew or casserole. It always made me feel hungry. This mixture was ladled out into buckets and taken to feed the pigs.

I used to go with my Dad in his lorry to collect the swill from people's houses. In addition we would collect from the boats and the army transit camps, especially the one in the old oil mills in Limekiln Street. Here I found my second favourite smell and my first love. A catering sergeant took a fancy to me, especially my curly hair. He used to call me 'Curly Shirley'. Each week he would make me a tray of 'DOSH'. This was rich, dark, treacly toffee. What a blessing it was to me to help stretch my sweet coupons. Oh! – how I loved that man – and I was all of five years old! They say that the way to a man's heart is through his stomach. I consider it to be the other way round.

I have only to smell a stew or a casserole cooking or toffee being made and my mind and my nose play tricks on me and can easily imagine that I am five years old again.

THE END OF THE WAR IN DOVER

Dawn Vaughan

DURING THE EARLY YEARS of the war, when I was about four years old, my parents decided to take me on a brief visit to Kent. I was left with my aunt and uncle who lived in Lydden, as Dover was considered to be too dangerous for children. However, my father collected me by car and took me for a short visit to see my grandparents who lived in the town.

As we lived in Oxfordshire, many miles from the sea, I was quite determined to 'see the sea' during the visit. I am told that I made such a fuss that in desperation my father drove down to the sea front, put me under his arm and ran along the promenade with me yelling in protest that I wanted to go on the beach.

I can remember very clearly seeing great rolls of barbed wire all along the sea front. It was a beautiful sunny day and the beach was almost deserted but in the sky vast numbers of barrage balloons were floating above Dover.

*   *   *   *

My parents and I moved to Dover in 1944 immediately after VE Day. We came from a delightful little Cotswold village, full of children and life and untouched by the war. While we were looking for a house in Dover we stayed with my paternal grandparents in Clarendon Place. My grandfather was a train driver. Throughout the war and after the war he drove the *Golden Arrow*.

My first impressions of Dover were of absolute horror and disbelief. In fact for months I used to go to bed and pray that it was just a bad dream and that I would wake up back in Witney.

Defending the shore. Defences at East Cliff, Dover.
Photograph by courtesy of the Imperial War Museum

Everything in Dover was either flattened or falling down. Most of the children were still away, having been evacuated, and very few schools in the area were operating. I went to Barton Road School, where there were very few children, I think initially about eight or ten of us. There was a formidable but kind headmistres called Miss Parkinson.

My parents bought a house in Leyburne Road, previously occupied by two Miss Hardys, said to be related to Captain Hardy, of Nelson fame. Most of the houses here were bomb damaged, some abandoned or demolished altogether. Our house had no electricity and it still had the bells in the kitchen to summon servants and the most enormous kitchen range we had ever seen. A grape vine growing in the conservatory almost covered the back of the house, so a great deal of work had to be done before we could move in. While clearing the garden my father unearthed a very ancient pot, complete with handles. (The curator of the museum at the time said it was an Eastern Urn, East Mediterraean, Grecian or Turkish, AD400-500). What a find!

My maternal grandmother's house stood in Liverpool Street, where the swimming pool is now. My mother used to send me to buy bread at Hopper's Bakeries, which stood in a sea of rubble, behind the sea front and near to the derelict Burlington Hotel. How the bakery survived I cannot imagine but the bread it produced was wonderful and by the time I got home there was usually a hole in the middle where I had been nibbling at it.

Riding my bike behind the sea front I could see rats running in the rubble. Some houses were still half standing and furniture and curtains were plainly visible in rooms with no roofs and with half the walls missing; extremely dangerous and a great temptation to children.

Soon the families returned to Dover and things improved. My friends and I played on the rocks under the Prince of Wales Pier, swam out to rafts strategically placed acoss the harbour and spent our pocket money on exciting speed boat trips from the beach. I soon forgot the Cotswold village and became the DOVORIAN that I am happy and proud to be.

PART 5

THE SECOND HALF
OF THE CENTURY
1951– 2000

INTRODUCTION

PART FIVE

The Second Half of the Century
1950 - 2000

THE LAST SECTION of this book is very different from the other four parts. One of the reasons for this lies in the fact that when members contributed to a series of articles entitled 'Memories of Dover' they wrote, as most people would, about early childhood memories. The only exception, which appears here in Part Five, is Edna Littlehales *First Impressions of Dover* in 1957, which tells of the gradual re-building of the town in the decade following the 1939-45 War.

We also chose to include an article by Nan Wheeler about the history of the Minerva Orchestra, which she joined in 1947. Her personal memories of the orchestra span the second half of the century.

After including these two pieces, we had many choices. We wanted to give our readers some glimpses of Dover in the second half of the century but we wanted the articles to be, as those in the rest of the book, people's personal memories or views. This posed a dilemma, as most of the Newsletter articles relating to the last fifty years were not written in this style. Another consideration was to select from all the events of these fifty years. We decided, after much discussion, to choose topics which had been reported in the Newsletter, were written by members and, where possible, we tried to choose items which had some relevance to the work of the Society. As the reader will perceive, this approach has resulted in a variety of offerings.

One of our first choices was from 1994, Bob Ratcliffe's, *The Closing of Marine Station, A Valediction* , accompanied by Alan Ashman's *The Golden Arrow*. This topic referred back to earlier descriptions of the station in E.J.Baker's article in Part Three. It then seemed logical to follow this with an account of the opening of the new Cruise Terminal in 1996 and complete the section with a description of the installation, at the terminal, of a Plaque to the Unknown Warrior in 1997, reported by Terry Sutton.

Our second choice was to report the Society's role in the moving of the Rolls Statue, in 1995, to its original site albeit in different surroundings in front of the Gateway flats. The story was told in two different *Newsletter* articles.

Another decision was to report the discovery of the Bronze Age Boat in 1992, and its subsquent return to Dover in 1999 to be installed in its new gallery at the Dover Museum. We have two articles by Keith Parfitt, of the Kent Archaeological Trust, on the discovery and recovery of the boat and then a final word from Christine Waterman, Curator of Dover Museum, on the opening of the gallery in Dover. In 2000 the Dover Society unveiled a plaque to mark the spot where the boat was discovered. This was part of its Millennium Project on Historic Plaques.

This led us to include a short report from Sheila Cope on the Society's project and choice of historic sites for the plaques.

The section ends with reports from Terry Sutton and Merril Lilley on the Millennium celebrations in Dover on 31st December 1999 and 1st January 2000, an appropriate end to these recollections of the century.

FIRST IMPRESSIONS
OF DOVER

E. M. LITTLEHALES

WE CAME TO DOVER in 1957 because my husband had obtained a post here. The summer had been very hot and sunshine continued into the autumn. We knew something of the town, having lived in Deal for a short time before the war, but the family had only glimpsed it from a train. After living in a village in the Medway valley for eighteen years, it was a great change – would it be a continuous seaside holiday? The bare downland, dramatic cliffs, the narrow streets, the traffic, trains, boats, and above all, the sea – ever colourful and changing – were most exciting. We enjoyed the wind and the invigorating air, so much recommended in Victorian times. One of the family had bronchial asthma, but not a single attack occurred after our move.

Most war damaged buildings were repaired or demolished. The site of the Gateway was flat with a huge crane and pile-drivers at work. Part of Townwall Street was still a narrow lane with various shops in use. That strange building, the Dover Stage, was just completed and prompted much discussion. Some elegant Victorian terraces climbed from Maison Dieu Road to Victoria Park, looking smart with new paint. The east and west sides of the Market Square were nearly rebuilt. The Front was neat, with bright flower beds, and the little steam train, preceded by its man with a red flag, puffed gently along. There was always something interesting to watch – the ferries, large and small yachts and, with no swimming bath, much sea swimming stimulated by a renewed interest in Channel swimming.

One could picture Dover as the important military place it had been. Barracks, officers' quarters, married quarters, a hospital, a church – some damaged and nearly all empty – dominated the skyline, especially on the

Western Heights. The Castle was still partly manned and kept spruce by the Army. As one wandered around the precincts, it was fun to come face to face with a marching 'squad', and to peep into the various workshops tucked into the walls, used by army craftsmen for repairs.

Nearby Connaught Park, with its beautiful views, was immaculately kept with sloping lawns, a large pond with goldfish, brilliant carpet bedding including the 'topiary' models of the Teddy Bear's Picnic – rather far from the town centre, but well worth the climb or a bus ride.

We had difficulty in finding a house, and as we had rented before, we had little money to buy one. There was a lull in private building. Some new

Pre-fabs on Buckland Estate

council houses had been built, and a number of 'pre-fabs' were still in use, but the Housing Department indignantly refused to help us, even temporarily, as we had 'chosen' to come to Dover. However, there was a number of older houses which had been in multiple occupation immediately after the War, and were now on the market, in poor condition. Having no car we had to consider bus services, which were good on the main roads – and fares which were quite low, 1d (2½p) from the Trough to the Post Office. Eventually we found a Victorian terrace house and obtained a mortgage. It needed much improvement but we had more space than ever before and it was within walking distance of the town centre and some schools.

At that time schools, old or new, were very crowded with the 'bulge' and in need of improvements, extensions and general modernisation. Some were borrowing rooms in other buildings or using cloakrooms and corridors for classes. Several new schools were planned but none were being built. There were few private schools.

An official told us that Dover was widely known for its many small shops and we were amazed by the number and diversity in that street-of-many-names and in the residential area. All the well-known grocery chains had a branch there. There were butchers and bakers galore, each with his own special line – a large Woolworths, still expanding, about twenty

Hatton's drapery and departmental store in Biggin Street.

chemists, five largish furnishers, china shops, excellent ironmongers and electricians, four good drapers, Hattons being the largest (anything unobtainable there could be done without). There were Co-op branches, selling nearly everything, all over the town and its suburbs. In fact one did not need to go elsewhere to buy any necessity. Dover was, perhaps, short of teashops but had a large number of public houses, many of which have now vanished.

York Street and The Lanes were shabby but still in use. The Western Docks, the Marine Station and the Pier District were undergoing changes

but were very busy, though local families were moving to the Aycliffe Estate. The huge gasworks were fully in use and Dover was very 'gas-minded'.

The town as a whole looked clean and the streets were swept regularly. Public gardens were kept trim and bright. There were enough well-kept 'conveniences', most with an attendant, and every scrap of metal on their doors was polished till it glittered. There was a lot of traffic, especially army vehicles and car transporters; it kept moving and there was much less parking than today. The flocks of roof-nesting seagulls spoiled the tidy picture but supplied a regular topic for the local press. On a wet day a downpour always caused cascades from shop roofs on to pavements and puddles everywhere – a problem still not solved.

We missed some country things – there were few large trees before the River area but the chalkland flowers were a joy – many vetches, valerian, vipers bugloss, scabious and lots of 'Alecs'. There was much to be explored on the beach and shells, fossils, flints and seaweeds to be collected. No wonder geology was a popular subject in schools!

To newcomers there seemed to be plenty of leisure activities – four cinemas, several recreation grounds, miniature golf courses, cricket and football pitches and active organisations such as Scouts, Guides, church clubs and very good dramatic and music societies. There were many evening classes with low fees. Churches of most denominations were active; a number have gone now.

Dover was – and still is – a family-based town. And the real Dovorians? Polite, yes, but very wary of newcomers.

The
MINERVA ORCHESTRA
1925-1999

NAN WHEELER

I N 1925 MR.FRED SEELEY, well known in Dover for his musical prowess, in particular with the cello, decided to form a small group of musicians to give concerts for charities and to play at local functions. They met each week to rehearse at the home of one of the members - in Minerva Avenue. Thus the Minerva Orchestra was launched.

By 1930 the group was well established with six regular players, with Fred Seeley as conductor: Mr. Gough as leader, Fred Burch, second violin, Jessie Husk, pianist, Mr. Taylor, flute, and Stan Coles, first violin. Numbers increased and the group twice changed venues. In the same year the Highland Light Infantry came to town and so many army bandsmen joined the group that they had to move again to larger premises in Husk's Yard. This was the peak time of the group's existence, when a thirty-strong orchestra gave many concerts.

Sadly, by 1932, the conductor had gone, the bandsmen had moved and the orchestra shrank. It gained several new members, however: Daisy West (then Sawyer) who played first violin; Don Bailiff, who played the viola, violin, double bass or sang, Les Bailiff, violin or piano and Mrs. Beach, violin. C. Dowler took over as leader from Mr. Gough. This smaller group continued giving concerts at many venues including the Brotherhood, Sisterhood, St. Mary's Church, St. Martin's Church and performed at civic and other functions. Some of the members, including Daisy West, joined a mandolin group, which gave weekly concerts on Dover sea front.

From 1939-46 conditions in Dover made it impossible for the group to continue. Most of the men left to serve their country. However, in 1946

Fred Seeley soon got the Minerva on its feet again, with a trio meeting in
Don Bailiff's house in River one week and Fred Seeley's house the next.
Playing out consisted of civic functions again, dinners, banquets and a
few charity events.

It became a quartet in 1947, when I joined the group, playing violin, as
did Don Bailiff. Les Bailiff played the piano, with Fred back on the cello.
More engagements were undertaken and the fee split among the players.
There were also many more charity performances. Happy days!

Once again numbers started to grow. By the end of 1948 we were meeting
at the home of Charlie Hedgecock in London Road, River. Charlie and his
son, Mike, played violins and Charlie's cousin, Bill, led the orchestra, after
Mr. Dowler, who had hoped to rejoin, sadly was unable to do so because of
rheumatism. Stan Coles and Daisy West came back. Concerts were given
more frequently and further afield. In fact we travelled anywhere on any
day, as long as transport was provided.

Some members of the Minerva Orchestra at River School, 1951.
Left to Right - Back Row: Messrs Sutton, Hedgecock, Jnr., Hedgecock, Snr., Gourlay, Brett, Challis,
Ashley. Middle Row: Messrs Birch, Dowler, Fuller, L. Bailiff, Coles, Wilsher. Front Row: Hedgecock
(Leader), Wheeler (Mrs), Sawyer (Mrs), Seeley (Conductor), Dowler (Mrs), D. Bailiff (Organiser).

The Minerva Orchestra at a concert in St. Richard's School in 1972.

With the return of Fred Burch we had to move again. In River Village Hall it seemed as if new players turned up every week. By now we had brass and woodwind players joining and we went to River School to rehearse.

Over the next few years we had many more new members. In 1948 Frank Fuller, a great character, joined us. He played the 'cello and did violin repairs for us. His father was a listed violin maker in London and Frank had his tools. In 1949 we gained the most colourful character, the clarinettist, Sam Bateman, who had played for many years in London theatres. Although he was well over seventy he cycled to our practices and local concerts. Also he looked after our stands and other equipment, repairing and maintaining them for the next ten years.

We played for pantomimes, musicals and orchestral concerts and found we had insufficient time left to practise and plan new programmes. It was difficult for most of us to spare more than two nights a week: many of our concerts were annual or twice-yearly: the alms-houses in Dover, Eastry Hospital, most Dover churches, carol concerts and homes for the aged in Kearsney and Dover.

1953 was Coronation Year and the Minerva Orchestra rose to the occasion with a Grand Coronation Concert in the Co-operative Hall, Maison Dieu Road Dover, on Wednesday, 15th April, at 7.30 pm. We had a complement of 22. There were six first violins, five second violins, 'cello,

double-bass, clarinet, trombone, trumpet, percussion and pianoforte. The conductor was Fred Seeley and the leader Bill Hedgecock. The vocal solos were by Don Bailiff, who was the secretary, and the trumpet solos by Fred Crane. In the following years the orchestra continued to meet in River but changed meeting places several times. Fred Seeley who had long wanted to play more cello left the Minerva and joined Dover Orchestra. He was sorely missed. Then Bill Hedgecock retired as leader due to ill health. Various leaders took over for short periods. I led for a while as a stop gap when I returned from overseas. Then when I moved away again Don Bailiff came to the rescue and conducted and George Peters took over as leader.

Concerts were given at many local venues and by 1961 we had twenty members on our lists and were meeting in Shatterlocks Primary School. Tony Marples came along with his French horn and was a real asset. From 1963 to 1967 we had several changes and additions to the orchestra. In 1968 John Hainsworth re-catalogued and filed all our music, no mean task with over 300 pieces. In 1972 Frank Fuller's wife, Eva, came and played the piano. She was a really wonderful accompanist and was much in demand in Kent.

In 1972 Les Bailiff died, a bitter blow for the orchestra who had relied on his knowledge and hard work. Then, after returning from a long holiday in South Africa, Don Bailiff died, yet another difficult place to fill. We had to spread the work around. Mr. Reg Franklin was our new conductor. We were playing at a lot more schools at this time. Then the cost of hiring halls became an overriding factor and for this reason we moved to Deal Secondary School for our rehearsals and also became affiliated to the Evening Institute.

In 1975 we were fifty years old and celebrated by giving a concert of light orchestral music in St. George's Hall, Deal, on St. George's Day with George Peters as leader and myself as deputy. When Reg Franklin resigned, George Peters became conductor and I became leader. Tony Marples was Secretary and Linda Hayward Treasurer. We had fewer players and gave fewer concerts. When Dover Orchestra had to close we gained as some of their players joined the Minerva.

The next major change came with the sudden death of George Peters, who had given us unselfish service since 1962. His musical knowledge and feeling for orchestral expression enabled us to reach our potential with concerts which enhanced our reputation.

In 1980 we gave a present of an engraved hip flask to Stan Coles to commemorate his membership of 50 years. He took on the difficult job of librarian and general adviser and, with our help, he checked through every set of music!

Daisy West died just before she completed 50 years service with the orchestra. Stan Coles survived only a few more years. In a short time we lost two of our first violins. In the following years there were many changes in all sections, with people moving away, or being too busy, or retiring. Our concerts had to be curtailed. At times we split up and at Deal Music Festival in 1983 the string section and woodwind section played separate items.

In 1984 we gave two concerts: one at Eastry Hospital, a regular venue, and one at Dover Methodist Hall, our favourite old haunt.

Since then there have been many players of all sorts and with all shapes of instruments who have come along for a few weeks or years and left for various reasons. There have also been many 'friends' who will help for a concert but who cannot attend regularly because of other commitments, but on the whole we manage to maintain a balance. Mention must be made of our soloists. We have been able to call on some very fine vocalists from the East Kent area who have given their services free.

Now, in 1999, seven of us still meet in East Studdal and play for our own enjoyment. We choose to play in the afternoons, as we are all retired. Two years ago I celebrated my 50 years with the orchestra and Tony Marples is still with us as Secretary/Treasurer.

DOVER MARINE
A Valediction
BOB RATCLIFFE

EDITOR'S NOTE: *The station's heyday was the period between the wars, when it was probably the most famous railway terminal outside London, synonymous with the adventure of foreign travel, epitomised by the Golden Arrow. When the station reopened after being used as a clearing house for troops during the Second World War the Golden Arrow service was restarted. The Golden Arrow was taken out of service in 1972 although boat trains continued to run until 1980. The station, by this time renamed Western Docks, gradually declined until it finally closed on 25th September 1994, which prompted these memories from Bob Ratcliffe and Alan Ashman.*

THE 24th SEPTEMBER 1994 HAD BEEN A GREY DAY, and a grey Channel was gently heaving under a grey sky. As I made my way along the elevated approach to Dover's Admiralty Pier, from the footbridge to the entrance to the station the strains of '*Tipperary*' assailed the ear, as if from a distant place – or time. The great station below me appeared almost deserted, save for a single electric multiple unit and a small gathering at the far end of platform 4. Other songs from the Kaiser's war drifted past, from the time when this station was new and when it served, not as the planned pride and joy of the South Eastern & Chatham's continental service, but as a vital casualty clearing post dealing with the countless wounded from the Western Front. How many more names would have been inscribed in the memorials to that terrible conflict had not the Marine Station replaced the original and entirely inadequate open jetty, and been available just in time to expedite rapid clearance of ambulance trains taking the wounded to the care of hospitals inland. In the mind's eye the deserted station became a scene of urgent action, with ambulance trains in every platform and the platforms themselves crowded with medical attendants and stretcher parties.

I wandered along the platform, past a small collection of sales stands that had anticipated some trade from those who had come to pay their last respects and relive past memories, past the small choir who were now chatting to the be-chained Mayor, past the rows of trolleys that had carried their last luggage 'aux les paquebots'. The sign had gone, and the great doorway to the quay stood open and unguarded – gone also were the policemen and the immigration officer – so I wandered out on to the quay, deserted, damp and grey on that September afternoon. Deserted now but how much pomp and circumstance had that quay witnessed in its eighty years? Monarchs, presidents, state visits, and it was here that the Unknown Warrior and Nurse Cavell were brought, finally returning home in the days following the end of the war to end all wars.

Dover Marine, seen from St. Martin's Battery on the cliffs above Snargate Street in 1979

In lighter vein I recalled a recently discovered photograph of that same quay, portraying a youthful *Maid of Kent* loading the mails for Calais. Poor doomed *Maid of Kent,* built in 1926 and with a stern that seemed to epitomise the age of short skirts and the Charleston, but soon, as a hospital ship, to be blasted into oblivion at Dieppe at the start of the Second World War. And then there were all the other Channel Packets that made this quay their home – *Empress, Riviera, Isle of Thanet, Canterbury, Invicta* – and the Belgians as well, the princes – *Charles, Leopold, Phillippe, Baudouin* – and so on until the last of them, *Princess Paola,* for I cannot count the remains of the lovely *Reine Astride,* her bow and stern cut off by an uncaring Belgian shipyard to form a truncated base for the

A foreign dignatory is met on arrival at Dover Marine, circa 1930.

'Maid of Orleans', 'Invicta', RTM 'Reine Astrid" and SNCF 'Côte D'Azur'
alongside the Admiralty Pier, Dover, in August 1972'.

hydrofoils that replaced the classic fleet, and the last ship to lie at this quay. And now they were all gone, and the only visible memory is the name of one – *Invicta* – painted at one of the mooring bollards in anticipation of mooring ropes that will never come.

Across the grey harbour at the Prince of Wales Pier lay a ship of the Grey Funnel LINE. HMS *Southampton* was visiting Dover and was lying at the berth that had once played host to trans-Atlantic liners. I remembered my first visit to Dover Harbour, full then of other grey ships at a time when recording such detail was frowned upon, and when my childish drawing of LCTs and MTBs was spirited away at the request of a naval officer!

And then there was another vision of more traumatic days of early June, 1940, when the harbour was full of vessels of all types and sizes and destroyers and paddlers alike were lying three or four abreast at the quay as the troops that they had brought out of Dunkirk made their way to the waiting troop specials in the great station. Sounds drifted into the mind, sounds of steam, and windlasses taking in slack cables, of ship's telegraphs, of shouted orders and of marching feet. One voice became more insistent: "Are you waiting for transport, sir?" The voice of the Sergeant-Major materialised into that of a yellow coated security man. "We can't have people walking about on the quayside, sir. It's because of the lorries. They come along here very fast".

We stood in the doorway and chatted. "What time's *Invicta* due in?" I pulled his leg gently. "There won't be any more ships in here. They'll all go in and out on the other side – the Eastern Docks".

Most of the security men were ex-military, apparently, and employed by a private firm which was in turn employed by the Dover Harbour Board. We talked about Dover and the war. "There's still a notice in our office that says 'Walking Wounded Left: Stretcher Cases Right'".

Now that is something that should be better known, and preserved. That is part of history.

I wandered back into the station and paused at the South Eastern & Chatham Railway's memorial from the First World War, and – by means of an additional small plaque – the Southern Railway's memorial from the Second War. The SE&CR listed all 556 of their men by name, but their Southern comrades had to be content with a number – 626 – from a more anonymous age. But what better site could there be for such a memorial? The Brighton men had an engine to remember them, but only her nameplate now remains, away to the north, in the railway museum at York. The South Western men were remembered in the main entrance to the rebuilt Waterloo Station, which now, by a quirk of fate, has become very apposite, for it is the approach to the platforms of the new European Passenger

The S.E.C.R. War Memorial as seen from the Cruise Terminal Departure Lounge.

Service. But there could be no better site for such a memorial than that on the pier at Dover – the nearest part of our island to continental Europe, whence so many of those named departed, never to return. My security friend said that the memorial was to be dismantled, and re-erected at the Priory Station! I shudder at such a suggestion. The Memorial is not just a free-standing monument. It is the wall, the building, the setting. It would be small men indeed – men with no soul – who would tear such a gem out of such a setting. Better by far to plan for its future in-situ, and what a future there could be for Dover Marine if there were men of sufficient vision and enthusiasm in the town.

I read again the names of the South Eastern & Chatham men and saluted their memory. I gazed again at the Angel of Peace protecting the soldier and the sailor, and I retraced my steps along the now deserted platform. Gone were the little choir and the Mayor and the trade stands. Gone was the EMU on its way to London via Chatham, in the wheel tracks of so many boat trains before it. No more 'Golden Arrows', no more 'Night Ferry', no more 'Continental Express – Short Sea Route'. The Channel Packet would henceforth play no part in reaching Europe now that Sir Alastair Morton had realised Sir Edward Watkins' dream. Henceforth a nonstop service could be offered via the tunnel. For the last time I climbed the steps to the footbridge and went out through the gates on to the original pier. Henceforth these gates would be locked and only the pigeons would be able to visit the Angel of Peace. Away to the westward the grey sea still heaved under the grey sky, lightened now by the invisible setting sun. The night shift of fishermen were arriving to take up their posts, sole occupants henceforth of a pier that had seen so much international activity for so long.

THE 'GOLDEN ARROW'

ALAN ASHMAN

I N THE EARLY POST-WAR YEARS the Marine Station came alive when the *Golden Arrow* train from Victoria arrived.

Porters lined Platform 3, baggage barrows at the ready, jostling for the privilege of carrying the luggage of the wealthy passengers to the ships.

The clever ones would have already positioned themselves exactly opposite the preordained position of the Pullman carriage doors and the more experienced porters could pile suitcases and trunks so high on the barrows that their visibility forwards was severely restricted, much against the orders so often repeated by the station master.

Once the passengers and porters had left the platform and disappeared into the Passport and Customs Halls a small army of cleaners appeared from behind the central buildings to take up their allotted tasks.

A gang of ladies, led by a redoubtable lady charge-hand, entered the train with assorted brooms, brushes, pails, dustpans and cleaning and polishing cloths and would not emerge again until the interior of the coaches were shining as new.

Another gang, mostly men, went to work on the exterior brass handles and brass step edges, while others cleaned and polished the windows and sides of the carriages.

The locomotive was moved to the loco sheds for the special attention of a select band of cleaners, firemen, etc. who proceeded to return the engine to a pristine state. Later in the afternoon the loco was run back to the Marine Station to head up the sparkling train of Pullman coaches

The arrival of the S.S. *Canterbury* or *Invicta* with the inwards service from Calais once again set the station alight with activity.

For many years a Pullman Car Inspector travelled on the ship from France and during the voyage contacted the most important passengers, whose identities were well known to the ship's officers, and this inspector took details of special arrangements for their reception at Victoria Station. Details were passed to the resident Pullman Car Inspector, who then pro-

The Golden Arrow

ceeded to the B.R. switchboard and relayed the relevant information to Victoria. This detailed the location of the VIPs on the train, the coach name, etc. so that the Rolls-Royce or Bentley could be parked alongside the arrival platform in the nearest position to enable these special passengers to walk only a short distance.

Truly a first-class service!

A TOUR OF
THE CRUISE TERMINAL

MERRIL LILLEY

T HE OFFICIAL OPENING of the Cruise Terminal at Dover took place
on 20th June,1996, and more than 200 guests attended and were
greeted by Jonathan Sloggett, Managing Director of Dover Harbour
Board. The Cunard *Royal Viking Sun* was in the port for the occasion and
the opening ceremony was performed by Peter Ward, Chairman and Chief
Executive of Cunard. He unveiled a plaque set between two photographs,
one of the *Golden Arrow* and one of the *Viking Sun.*

Part of the Departure Lounge at the Cruise Terminal.

The parking area at the Cruise Terminal.

However, cruise ships had been using the terminal since April, 1996, and some local people had been fortunate enough to get a tour of the terminal before the official opening in June. Among these were a large number of Dover Society members who, on Saturday, 11th May, attended the annual Spring Conference of the Kent Federation of Amenity Societies, hosted by the Dover Society.

After a morning of talks and an excellent lunch, two large coaches left for an afternoon tour of the Eastern and Western Docks. At the Western Docks the coach party visited the Cruise Terminal – a treat indeed to be the first local visitors to be allowed a glimpse inside. As there was a cruise ship in port each visitor was issued with a special red sticker to enable the party to pass through port security, feeling very conscious that this was a first occasion.

We passed beneath the entrance canopy, through the check-in hall, up the gleaming escalator to the departure lounges, exclaiming as we went on the fantastic transformation of the old Marine Station into this attractive and spacious international cruise location, where liners leave for Scandinavia, the Baltic or the Mediterranean and beyond. Passengers embarking at Dover pass this way and pause in the comfortable lounge to view the magnificent arching spines of the old station and the re-furbished splendour of the Southern Railway's Memorial from the First World War.

The old railway lines have been covered in and the area where trains arrived at crowded platforms is now a useful car park for cruise passengers.

We met some passengers returning to the ship after walking into Dover and we were anxious to know their impressions of the town. A couple from Michigan, USA, said they thought it was a nice little town to visit. They had wanted to go to the castle but had not left themselves enough time. They had lunched at Dickens' Corner and done some shopping. They were very enthusiastic about English greetings cards and had bought some from the Gift Box in Bench Street, particularly one for a Golden Wedding. They thought all the people in the town were very friendly. We saw them walk on to the gangway to resume their cruise and wished we could join them.

The Royal Viking Sun.

THE PLAQUE
to the
UNKNOWN WARRIOR

TERRY SUTTON

I N 1997 THE DOVER SOCIETY was praised for its initiative in providing the plaque that marks the spot where, in 1920, the body of World War One's Unknown Warrior was landed in his homeland. The Society had received a number of requests that this important event should be recorded for posterity and after discussions with the War Graves Commission and the Western Front Veterans' Association the committee was able to arrange for the erection of a suitable plaque which, wrought in Portland stone, measures 20ins x 10 ins.

> Near this spot on the 10th November 1920
> the body of the Unknown Warrior
> was brought ashore from HMS Verdun
> on the way to its final resting place
> at Westminster Abbey.
>
> The Dover Society 1997

The plaque was fixed to the wall of the new cruise terminal reception office where it would be seen by all embarking passengers.

Praise for the Society came from the Chief of the Defence Staff, General Sir Charles Guthrie, when he unveiled the plaque at a ceremony at the terminal in the old Marine Station in May. Other senior Army officers joined with the Mayor, Councillor Lyn Young, representatives of Dover Harbour Board and of the Dover Society, to watch the unveiling ceremony.

The Society's vice-chairman, John Gerrard, opening the proceedings, introducing Alistair Lawton of Deal, the deputy chairman of Dover Harbour Board. Mr. Lawton welcomed the guests and pointed out that two members of the Society present that day were alive in Dover when the Unknown Warrior was landed in November 1920 - Miss Lillian Kay and Budge Adams.

The Chairman, Jack Woolford, explained to the visitors that the Dover Society aimed to be a constructive organisation and, among other duties, commemorated historic events. He said that it was David Atwood, a Society member, who came forward with the idea of the plaque for the Unknown Warrior and the committee gladly took it up. Mr. Woolford thanked Dover Harbour Board for its assistance and generosity in carrying through the project to its fruition. He said the plaque recorded a unique occasion in Dover's history.

Sir Charles Guthrie recalled that 908,000 servicemen from the British Empire were killed in World War One. Wars continued, he said, with 31 major conflicts in progress at that time. Memories of those who died in war should, he said, make men redouble their efforts to bring about world wide peace.

Sir Charles also thanked the town of Dover for its continuing links with the military, links that went back hundreds of years before the Crusaders, and thanked the Dover Society for persuing Mr Atwood's suggestion.

The Reverend Graham Batten, Vicar of St. Mary's and Honorary Chaplain to Dover Harbour Board, led prayers at the ceremony and a representative of the British Legion laid a wreath before the sounding of the Last Post and Reveille by a member of the Parachute Regiment stationed at Dover.

How the remains of the Unknown Warrior were selected makes an interesting story, somewhat hidden in myths and rumours that have gathered around the event.

At first the idea of a tomb for an Unknown Warrior in Britain was not well received – the French already had a similar idea for Paris – but eventually King George V gave his consent and the orders went out to senior British officers in France.

Groups of British soldiers, each under an officer, went, independently and secretly, to four of the biggest battlefields - Aisne, Arras, Somme and Ypres -where crude wooden crosses marked where Tommies were buried.

Each group, armed with shovels and a sack, located a cross that indicated that the identity of the soldier was not known. In each case the remains were exhumed, placed in the sack and taken by field ambulance to a temporary chapel at St. Pol in northern France.

The four sets of remains were guarded there overnight and next day a high-ranking British officer - some reports say he was blindfolded – entered the chapel and touched one of the bodies, all of which were covered by Union flags.

That one body, inside a plain coffin, was taken to Boulogne, where its last resting place in France is marked by a plaque. With the coffin went sacks of soil dug from the spot where the soldier had died, so that the earth of France that he was defending would cover the warrior's last resting place in Westminster Abbey.

On 10th November 1920 the body, still wrapped in the sack and in the plain coffin, was placed in a larger oak coffin designed and presented by the Undertakers' Association. Then, with great ceremony, it was taken aboard the British warship, HMS *Verdun*, which sailed from Boulogne to Dover. HMS *Verdun*, selected because its name honoured battlefield bravery of the French, was escorted across a mist-shrouded Channel by six destroyers.

At Dover people lined the cliffs and other vantage points to see the Unknown Warrior return home. At the Admiralty Pier representatives of the nation were waiting and Dover's civic leaders were among those there to pay homage. With great ceremony the warrior's coffin and the sacks of soil were loaded into a baggage van and taken by railway through Kent where people lined the track all the way to London. Next day the remains were carried in procession through the streets to be finally laid to rest at Westminster Abbey on 11th November 1920.

And so the man who is buried among kings at the Abbey could have been anyone – one of the gentry, a professional soldier, a factory worker, even a rogue. But whoever he was he represents all those hundreds of thousands of British troops who died for their country but whose identities are unknown except to God.

Information gleaned from the *Dover Express,* other newspapers and books, including *The Story of the Unknown Warrio*r by Michael Gavaghan.

Editor's Notes:

1. The above piece is a condensed version of different articles by Terry Sutton which appeared in Newsletters in 1996 and 1997.

2. For an eye witness account of the arrival of the Unknown Warrior in Dover see the first article in Part 'Two of this book.

MOVING THE ROLLS MEMORIAL
An Introduction to "A Spectator's View"

*These notes include passages from articles by Budge Adams, in Newsletter
No. 22, and by Terry Sutton and Jack Woolford, in* Newsletter *No. 23.*

EDITOR

O N FRIDAY 2 JUNE, 1995, the rededication of the memorial to Charles
Stewart Rolls took place on the Sea Front.

This ceremony was the successful culmination of a plan which
had been discussed since 1992, when Budge Adams and David Atwood
discovered that they shared a concern that the statue should be moved.
It was standing on a location on a wide area of the promenade at the root
of Boundary Groyne, which had been an appropriate site when, because
its original 1912 site on the Guilford Lawn had been severely war-damaged, it was placed there in about 1952. However, later a large public
convenience had been built behind it and many residents of Dover were
not happy with what Budge Adams described as "an almost insulting juxtaposition of these so dissimilar structures".

After three years of sustained discussion and correspondence the statue
was transferred to its new location on the lawns in front of the Gateway
flats. At the ceremony Jonathan Sloggett, Registrar and General Manager
of Dover Harbour Board, began the proceedings by thanking Impact and
the Rolls Royce Enthusiasts Club for their help and said that the Harbour
Board was pleased to have taken part in the move.

The Reverend Graham Batten, Vicar of St. Mary's and Chaplin to the
Port, dedicated the Memorial.

Mike Evans, Chairman of the Rolls Royce Heritage Trust, said that as
a life-long employee of Rolls Royce he was honoured by the invitation
to unveil the statue. He paid tribute to the Dover Society, the initiative
and persistence of Budge Adams's campaign and the help of John Gerrard,
Dover Harbour Board's Services General Manager, who unfortunately was
unable to attend. He also thanked Impact and Dover District Council for
making the site available and the Rolls Royce owners who had graced the
occasion with their cars.

The concept of the Rolls statue in Dover was to commemorate his
greatest achievement, his cross-Channel flight of 2 June 1910, the first
two-way, non-stop English Channel flight, just one year after Louis Bleriot's
pioneer Channel flight. These achievements alerted people to the significance of air travel and air power in the future, with Lord Northcliffe's
Daily Mail declaring, 'Britain is no longer an island'.

MOVING THE ROLLS MEMORIAL
A SPECTATOR'S VIEW

MAY JONES

A T 10.40 AM ON FRIDAY. JUNE 2ND, the first arrivals of the Rolls-Royce Enthusiasts Club were gliding effortlessly eastwards along Marine Parade. Fifteen minutes later a convoy of more than twenty vintage Rolls-Royces appeared, in close formation behind their police escort, from the opposite end of the Sea Front. From here they were marshalled, with due solemnity, on to the promenade facing the sea with their backs to the railings, which allowed the gathering crowd of Dovorians and visitors to admire the well kept exteriors and to chat to their owners.

Immediately after the re-dedication.

Alan Clark, suitably attired in sheepskin jacket to withstand the rigours of the English summer, was driving his pre-WW1 open-top model, still capable of coping with mountainous terrain, as its Alpine Rally Geneva 1993 plate triumphantly announced. Towards the other end of the line was a beautiful 1960 Silver Cloud 2, gleaming from its fortnightly polish and allowed out in the rain only if its journey was unavoidable. All the assembled vehicles were beautifully kept and made a fitting 'guard of honour' for the re-dedication of the Rolls statue on its granite plinth, surrounded

The Unveiling of the statue on Guilford Lawn, April 1912.   Photo by courtesy of Rolls-Royce plc.

by freshly-laid turf. In its new position, on the lawns in front of the Gateway flats at the western end, it is on almost exactly the same site as its original installation on Guilford Lawn in 1912.

Once the vehicles were in place the crowd awaited the arrival of the official party, composed of members from all the organisations which had contributed to the re-location of the statue: the Dover Harbour Board, the Dover District Council, Impact, Rolls plc and, above all, the Dover Society, represented on this occasion by Jack Woolford, Leo Wright and Budge Adams, the instigator of the event.

When all had taken their places, Jonathan Sloggett, of Dover Harbour Board, introduced the Rev. Graham Batten, Vicar of St. Mary's who performed the dedication by reading the passage from Ecclesiastes:

"Let us now praise famous men ... their bodies are buried in peace, but their name lives for ever more" and then offering a short prayer. Mr Michael Evans, Chairman of the Rolls-Royce Heritage Trust, officially unveiled the statue in its new position, before delivering a very interesting speech outlining the life of Charlie Rolls and the history of the foundation and work of the Rolls-Royce Company. At one point his words were almost drowned by the roar of Hovercraft engines (Rolls-Royce, of course!) as the vessel crossed the harbour on its way to its berth behind the Prince of Wales Pier.

The figure of Rolls and its simple inscription, sculpted by Kathleen Scott, the wife of the Antarctic explorer, now stands suitably located facing the Channel, where all can see and appreciate it.

Two hundred or so spectators present at the June 2nd ceremony were not only honouring the memory of its subject and indulging an interest in vintage vehicles, but also happily rejoicing with Budge Adams. Without his drive and perseverance the re-siting of the statue would not have taken place.

"an almost insulting juxtaposition of these so disimilar structures"

THE DISCOVERY
of the
BRONZE AGE BOAT

KEITH PARFITT

A BROAD SEQUENCE of archaeological evidence relating to the Mediaeval and post-Mediaeval town had been studied by the end of the summer of 1992 and the fieldwork phase of the operation appeared to be coming to a close, when a highly exciting find was revealed by the contractors working on the new underpass.

At lunch-time on Monday 28th September, (the 345th day of continuous fieldwork by the Canterbury Archeaological Trust) a team member spotted a group of substantial timbers in the bottom of a contractor's deep pit at the junction of Bench Street and Townwall Street, some six metres below ground level and just below Ordnance Datum. A rapid inspection indicated that these timbers formed part of a boat; moreover, the use of twisted withies within its construction, and the associated tufa and peats, suggested that the vessel could be prehistoric. Following a meeting with the consulting engineers, Mott Macdonald, and their main contractor, Norwest Holst, the remainder of the day was allowed for a fuller assessment of the extent and preservation of the vessel. It was soon obvious that the lower portion of the boat was intact, apart from the damage to one area already sustained during the machine excavations.

The initial investigations revealed that the timbers extended for some 6 metres across the full width of the pit and it became clear that we were dealing with the substantially complete mid-section of a very well preserved prehistoric plank-sewn boat, broadly similar to that found at North Ferriby before the last war, and obviously a crucial new find for nautical archaeology.

Numerous telephone calls and meetings the following day culminated in the grant of six days to excavate and record the remains fully. The ever-helpful engineers had already checked and indicated that, unfortunately, the levels could not be raised in order to preserve the boat *in situ.*

Since the boat would have to be removed to allow the contractors to excavate even deeper to complete their work, it was decided that the boat had to be lifted. A team of experts was hastily assembled to decide how this could be achieved. The main problem to resolve was whether to attempt the lift in one, or whether to cut the boat into sections and lift these individually. Opinions were divided, and remain so. However, it was generally agreed, due to the fairly fragile nature of its construction, the time factor and the damage already sustained, that it would be safer to cut the boat into manageable segments, thereby safeguarding key structural features.

Work on the boat continued for thirteen hours each day and by the Friday night all the recording had been completed ready for the lift on Saturday. Working in conjunction with English Heritage conservators, the

Lifting the first timbers of Dover's Bronze Age Boat.

Excavation of the second section.

boat was then cut into ten lettered sections each being manoeuvred on to a pallet and then removed from the excavation using a crane and lorry kindly supplied by Dover Harbour Board. At 5.30 pm on Saturday 3rd October the almost exhausted excavation team gave the signal to raise the final section of the boat which was then taken, by lorry, to join the other sections now resting in a large water tank previously prepared by the Harbour Board in one of its store buildings on the quay side only a short distance away.

The lifting operations were watched by a large crowd of Dovorians, eager to see the remains of the ancient vessel so appropriately discovered at one of Europe's most famous ports. The atmosphere was somewhat akin to the homecoming of the Mary Rose to Portsmouth!

From the details of its construction, the craft must have been the product of a master boat builder working within a long established tradition – the workmanship was superb, with cleats and central rails being carved from the two large oak base planks and held together by transverse timbers. The side planks were held in place by individual stitches of twisted yew wood with moss caulking between the joints.

During the following week the contractors resumed their construction work whilst the archaeological field-team correlated their somewhat hastily prepared notes and drawings. It was clear that further substantial sections of the vessel must lie to the north and south of the mid-section already lifted. Although these sections were beyond the limits of the contractor's excavations, fears increased regarding the effects of the new deep subway and its associated water pumping station on the surrounding water table. There seemed to be no certainty that if the remaining parts of the vessel were left *in situ* for future generations to excavate and study with improved techniques, the sediments would remain sufficiently waterlogged to allow the preservation of the boat timbers. Instructions were therefore issued by the Department of Transport and English Heritage to attempt to lift the remaining portions of the boat.

The close proximity of tall Victorian buildings immediately to the north precluded excavation here but a second coffer dam immediately to the south of the first was inserted and a further eight days allowed for the excavation of the southern section of the vessel.

The reward for the considerable amount of extra effort and cost put into the new excavation was the exposure of a further 3.5 metres of the craft including the remains of an original end - it was not clear whether this represented the bow or the stern. Interestingly, this had been partially dismantled soon after the boat was abandoned. A large section of the structure had been cut away, leaving intact the feathered ends of the side planks and the rather strange-looking forked terminal of the central base rails.

The same procedure was agreed for the lifting of the second section of the boat and this was undertaken on Monday, 19th October, in heavy rain, the final segment being retrieved at 8.45 pm. A total of 9.5 metres of the boat had now been raised, which was estimated to be about half to two-thirds of the total length. There seemed to be little doubt that the craft represented a sea-going vessel which presumably made regular trips across the Dover Straits.

The raising of the Dover boat proved to be a splendid example of co-operation and assistance by many different companies, official bodies and individuals. Substantial financial assistance was provided by English Heritage and the Department of Transport, whilst the engineers of Mott MacDonald and Norwest Holt gave invaluable practical help and encouragement on the site. Dover Harbour Board played a vital part in the actual lifting and storage of the vessel, whilst Dover Museum and Dover District Council provided essential back-up to the excavation team.

[cont overleaf

The Next Phase ...

WITH THE RECOVERY PHASE OVER the exhausted excavation team took a few days well earned rest before returning to carry out a more detailed consideration of just what had been found and the significance of it all. An open day was held for the country's leading experts in prehistoric and maritime studies and by the end of that day it was abundantly clear to all that a crucial find of international importance had been recovered. It soon became obvious to the excavators that the safe recovery of the vessel represented not so much the successful conclusion of the large-scale A20 project as the start of a massive study in prehistoric nautical archaeology. A detailed programme of research had to be devised and its funding agreed with English Heritage. Such an important find is naturally worthy of display but the stabilisation of water-logged wood is a notoriously long and difficult undertaking, thus a scheme for the treatment of the timbers and their eventual display to the public had to he considered. The full extent of the Dover Boat Project thus became all too clear.

Before anything could be done about conservation and display, how-ever, a detailed study of the recovered timbers was required in case they started to deteriorate and this was the main task over the next nine months. Based in the Harbour Board's store building with its two water tanks, a team of specialists spent many hours examining and recording every detail of the boat's structure. Led by Mrs Valerie Fenwick, one of the country's leading nautical archaeologists, experts examined the ancient wood for tool marks, details of the construction techniques and evidence for later repairs. Detailed fuII size drawings of the remains were prepared and numerous photographs taken.

In order to recover the remains of the boat it had been necessary to cut it up into manageable sections and although this decision had been somewhat reluctantly made, it made the subsequent handling and examination of the vessel considerably easier. The boat had been lifted 'right way up'; as a consequence no one had ever been able to examine its underside. Another aspect of the work, therefore, was to prepare special supporting cradles to allow the individual timber sections to be turned over and their underside drawn and examined. Still covered by an inch or two of original undisturbed river sediment, the cleaning of the bottom of the vessel yielded further samples of the material that was trapped under the boat when it was beached and one of the most interesting finds was

the articulated skeleton of a fish provisionally identified as a salmon.
Special new cradles of fibre-glass were constructed to replace the wooden boards used in the original lift. These were to support the timbers after their re-inversion.

As all this work began to draw to a close the next stage of the project—conservation – had to be carefully planned. It was thought that the work would take around eighteen months, which would give time to sort out future requirements for public display and allow the specialists to produce a detailed account of every aspect of the boat and its associated prehistoric landscape.

The Bronze Age Boat in its new gallery in Dover Museum

THE BRONZE AGE BOAT
A Curator's Tale
CHRISTINE WATERMAN

I FIRST MET THE DOVER BOAT on the 29th September 1992, the day after Keith Panfitt had discovered it only a few hundred yards from my office. I had been on leave on the previous day and I had barely opened the door to my office when Keith arrived to tell me about the find.

I was immensely sceptical. Having an archaeology degree myself, I knew that what he said he had found was very rare and often archaeological finds, although wonderful to an archaeologist, can be rather disappointingly partial, damaged or require a lot of interpretation and knowledge to be able to make them of interest to most people.

It was with a certain reluctance then that I accompanied him the few hundred yards to the end of Bench Street

I've been well served for that scepticism in the last seven years. My reaction to the first sight I had of the boat, looking down that deep and muddy hole was very physical, like an actual blow, as I took in the beauty and importance of what I could see.

It was as Keith had said, a stitched plank Bronze Age boat, largely intact and wonderfully preserved, lying just as it had been abandoned by our ancestors for 3,500 years.

I knew that Dover District Council would not be able to fund this project, then estimated at a total cost of £1 million. I hoped that they would let their museum staff support it and this they did, generously, for the following seven years, ultimately providing not only hundreds of hours of our time, thereby forgoing and delaying other important projects, but also gave a space and a 25 year commitment to finance the running of the gallery and its essential air conditioning.

Keith Parfitt has described how the boat was lifted and studied, throughout 1993. In October of that year Paul Bennett, Director of Canterbury Archaeological Trust, and I formed the Dover Bronze Age Boat Trust which was to become the owner of the boat and the driving force behind the project.

Our Trustees, all local, came from Dover's leading organisations and included the District Council, P&O European Ferries (now P&O Stena Line), Dover Harbour Board, George Hammond PLC and the Canterbury Archaeological Trust, whose Chairman, Dr. F.H. Panton, CBE, also became the Boat Trust's Chairman. The support of these organisations and individuals was to be critical throughout the next six years.

The Trust's first activity was to organise two open days to allow the public to view the timbers which only the archaeologists had seen until then. Three thousand people came to the 'boat shed' (now part of the successful De Bradelei Wharf shopping complex) in one weekend. A leaflet and booklet were published with the help of a Kent Archaeological Society grant and in May 1994 the Trust was launched at a reception on board the P&O ferry *Pride of Burgundy* when one piece of the boat made its first Channel crossing (six times!) for 3,500 years. At the reception, hosted by P&O, Sir Jocelyn Stevens, Chairman of English Heritage, pledged £300,000 towards the cost of preserving the boat.

By the following May the Trust had received full charitable status, had been gifted the boat by the Department of Transport and secured the approval of DDC to house it in a part of the White Cliffs Experience, then occupied by a restaurant and shop. Fund raising was now well under way with donations already totalling c.£350,000, whilst the major fundraising document, a £1.2 million application to the Heritage Lottery Fund, was in preparation.

In the meantime the boat had been moved, with the help of Dover Harbour Board, to tanks in the former army gym at Old Park Barracks, Whitfield. Here, for a year, it was to be soaked in a water soluble wax (polyethylene glycol) to impregnate the ancient wood with wax which would later be hardened by freeze drying. This later process would not only remove all the water from the timbers and allow them to be viewed in a dry state but give some strength to the wood's structure.

In August 1995 a team from the Mary Rose Trust and Canterbury Archaeological Trust, supervised by English Heritage, packed and sealed each timber carefully for its journey by refrigerated lorry to the Mary Rose laboratories in Portsmouth.

Paul Bennett and I travelled down to Portsmouth in advance of the lorry to see the first batch of timbers loaded into the MRT's large freeze dryer and to give interviews to the local and regional press. It was a bit of a wrench to see it leave Dover, but we fully expected to see it come back. In the event, it was to be three years before the timbers were to return to

Dover, whilst funds were secured and the gallery space was made ready.

In September 1996 we were delighted to hear that the Heritage Lottery Fund had approved a grant of £953,000 (later increased to £1.2 million), matched in February 1997 by a further £25,000 from the Wolfson Foundation and £55,000 from the European Regional Development Fund (KONVER Programme). We had hoped that HLF would provide an endowment fund to pay for the 24 hour air conditioning needed for the boat, but when they declined, Dover District Council agreed to meet these costs and, following a lengthy negotiation of contract details, the construction of the gallery finally began in May1998.

Only three months later the converted restaurant was ready to receive the boat and, with intense media coverage, the thirty two pieces were returned to Dover in August.

As we unwrapped the first piece there was some concern. Would it look good? Had it come through the process well? We need not have worried. The Mary Rose team had done a fantastic job.

The next part of the project, the reassembly of the timbers onto a special cradle, could commence. None of us, least of all Peter Clark from Canterbury Archaeological Trust who was to manage the re-assembly and Barry Corke and Adrian Murphy who were to spend a year on the work, underestimated the problems associated with this. The boat had been cut up in order to remove it safely from the ground. Now it had to be put back together, safely supported, but also presented as an exhibit in the most effective way. No-one had ever attempted to do such work before and with such a fragile, ancient and important artefact, re-assembly had to be carried out slowly and carefully. To add to their difficulties all of the work was carried out in the public eye, as viewing panels were installed in the protective panelling of the working 'envelope' to allow visitors to see the work in progress.

Whilst the reassembly was proceeding throughout 1998 and 1999 the museum staff, including myself, Jon Iveson, Elizabeth Owen, Mark Frost and Margaret Sharp worked with a team of specialists, including model makers, graphic designers, software designers, prehistoric hut builders and others, to prepare the final detailed designs for the gallery. Our principal gallery designer, Mike Whalley of Brennan & Whalley, had been associated with the project from 1996 when he drew up the outline gallery plans for the Trust's lottery bid.

We knew we had to try to explain not only the story of the boat but also the Bronze Age period which is so little known to most visitors.

We also knew that to engage people's interest we had to use as many interactive exhibits as possible. These were realised through the three computer interactives, the laboratory area and the jigsaw and a 'talking' hut label.

The computer software is a good example of the work involved in preparing the exhibition. The programme has $c.16,000$ words of text, hundreds of pictures, some games and video clips executed in five languages including English. Most of the pictures in the gallery were either commissioned specially or sourced from museum picture libraries and individuals all over the world.

The reassembly of the boat was completed in July 1999, followed by the final fit-out of the exhibition gallery, co-ordinated by Jenner, a Folkestone firm of builders who won both of the building tenders for the gallery. By 1999 they had gone fully 'native' and cared as much for the safety and care of the boat as the rest of the team.

On 22nd November, 1999 the Rt. Hon. Lord Kingsdown, Lord Lieutenant of Kent, opened the gallery in the presence of 120 guests, many of them members of a team which we estimate was made up of $c.150$ people who worked on the project. This was followed in March 2000 by a visit to the gallery by HRH The Prince of Wales.

Today the Dover Bronze Age Boat Gallery is an established feature of Dover's heritage attractions. It has also, to our great pleasure, brought many local people back to the museum or into it for the first time.

The aim of the Boat Trust, to preserve and display the boat in Dover where it was found, has been fully realised, and we are both very proud of the project and grateful for all the hard work and support that so many people and organisations have provided to make it happen.

THE DOVER SOCIETY'S MILLENNIUM PROJECT

Two Years of Planning: 1998-2000

SHEILA R. COPE

EVEN AS THE COMMITTEE ENTHUSIASTICALLY ENDORSED Terry Sutton's proposal that for its Millennium Project the Dover Society should erect ten commemorative plaques I had a premonition that there might be problems ahead. It took the last two years of the century accompanied by a sense of wading through treacle soup before the first plaques were installed in February 2000.

Initially our sub committee of Terry, Mike Weston and myself approached three local firms for estimates but none was able to produce, at an affordable price, a plaque of the type we had in mind, similar in style and quality to the blue plaques in London.

The Civic Trust provided the names of two manufacturers and a template was designed based on an oval shape because it was felt that it would be more elegant than a circle. At this stage the proposed lettering was simple block capitals, subsequently amended to upper case in a normal standard classic typeface as being more elegant. Lettering was to be white on a blue background, appropriate to a seaside town. Having been reassured that plaques made from cast aluminium would withstand the corrosive effects of Dover's salty air, we chose our supplier on the basis of price and recommendation, although the firm subsequently closed.

To create the greatest impact we planned to erect our first plaques centrally in the Market Square area. We met one rainy morning to decide where to place two of our first plaques, on Barclay's Bank (instruments of punishment) and on the TSB Bank (last shell to fall on Dover).

184   We had ascertained that planning permission was required only for listed
buildings – which these were not.

We spent many months dealing with applications and insurance. As it
turned out, one of the first plaques for which we obtained permission was
the one for the Bronze Age Boat, its position confirmed by Keith Parfitt
himself who happened to be walking through the underpass as we

Plaque installed at Lloyds TSB.   *Plaque installed at Taswell Street.*

discussed the location with Christine Waterman. Invitations were accepted
and everything arranged for this plaque to be installed on 11th December,
1999. We were pleased that the first plaque would be in place before the
year 2000. Then, about a fortnight before the planned ceremony, the
underpass was closed for an indefinite period and the installation had to
be postponed.

It became clear that each plaque would have its own particular
setback. With the 'first aerial bomb' plaque at Taswell Close, siting was the
problem, finally resolved through Hugh Gordon's approach to
Mr and Mrs Wicks who kindly accepted its installation on their property.
Imagine our relief, when, in brilliant sunshine on the morning of
February 16th, 2000, the first plaque was unveiled by the Town Mayor,
Mrs. Sansum.

It was followed, on February 19th, by the placing, on the Lloyds TSB
building in Castle Street, of the plaque commemorating the last shell to
fall on Dover, which was unveiled by Councillor Frank Woodbridge. It was
noteworthy that these two events were related to each other in the
context of Dover's history and that, at each installation, those who spoke
were directly connected to them by their own experience.

On April 17th the third and fourth plaques were unveiled, the third
marking the spot in the underpass where the Bronze Age Boat was
discovered and the fourth, in the Market Square, marking the spot where
convicted felons were punished.

This left six plaques still to be placed throughout the remainder of
the year 2000.

By August we had three more plaques on order. These were to be
placed in the following locations: – the Market Hall, at street level under
the now rebuilt Dover Museum, where those who fell in the Zeebrugge
Raid were brought, Camden Crescent, where Charles Dickens lodged while
he wrote Bleak House and Stembrook, where William Burgess, painter
and illustrator, lived. The last three plaques, each awaiting owner's
permission, were intended for the following places:– the crossroads at
Tower Hamlets, where Dover's gallows stood, Maritime House, Snargate
Street, on which site was born Philip Yorke, later Baron Hardwicke and
Lord Chancellor, and finally Lord Warden House, where Napoleon III was
reunited with his wife, Empress Eugenie, on his exile to England in 1871.

Thus have we planned to achieve our objective of placing the ten
commemorative plaques in the town as the Society's Millennium Project,
not by the end of 1999 but by the end of the year 2000.

MILLENNIUM CELEBRATIONS

Impressions of the Celebrations by two Members of the Dover Society

The Peacelight Lantern Procession and the Millennium Clock and Celebrating New Year's Eve, 1999

1. TERRY SUTTON

WHAT BETTER WAY to bid farewell to the old Millennium? More than three thousand happy faces, young and old, filled Dover Town Centre as they walked in a colourful Peacelight Lantern procession from Dover College to the Sea Front.

It was the spectacular New Year's Eve community event, superbly created by the Strange Cargo Arts Company, and the start of two days of Millennium celebrations. By the time the procession reached the Sea Front, through the Christmas illuminated and decorated streets, lined with spectators, there were more than five thousand people enjoying the magical scene.

The evening started, in the historic grounds of Dover College, with a service, for all denominations, organised by Christians Together in Dover. Then the procession set off. Children and parents carried hundreds of simple but beautiful lanterns made in free local workshops around the Dover area. The lanterns were lit by a flame that had started as the Peace Light in Bethlehem and had been carried across Europe by Scouts, including those from Dover.

The procession slowly made its way out of the College, led by the infectious rhythms of the brilliant Busker Du Street-Band of Folkestone,

One of the displays in the Carnival Procession, 1st January, 2000.

which proved a big hit with those taking part and with the hundreds lining the streets.

At that point, leaving the College, Dover District Council took over from Christians Together to run the event in a special partnership scheme. The cavalcade went through the pedestrian precinct to the Market Square, along Castle Street, Russell Street, Townwall Street and through Wellesley Road to the Sea Front.

On the Sea Front promenade the huge crowd watched a large sculptural bonfire on the beach as the Clock of the Second Millennium creaked in flames through its final minutes into a new age. A variety of colours lit up the clock as the weight of centuries of human experience drove the clock into its final celebratory moments of the twentieth century. It was accompanied by film slides of the ages past. Intriguing, thought-provoking music was composed by Peter Cook of Canterbury.

The exciting event ended in a cacophony of sound, flashing lights and a fantastic display of fireworks. The Second Millennium was no more... but the Third Millennium was waiting to arise from the bonfire ashes on New Year's Day.

Carnival of the Planets and the 3rd Millennium Clock,
New Year's Day, 1st January 2000

2. MERRIL LILLEY

T HE SECOND EVENING of the Millennium celebrations again
started from Dover College grounds, this time in the form of a
Mardi Gras style carnival with ten sections of the procession, each
representing one of the planets of the solar system led by the sun. The

Carnival Procession, 1st January, 2000.

route of the procession was, as on the previous day, through Effingham
Crescent, Biggin Street, Cannon Street, Market Square, Castle Street, Townwall Street and Wellesley Road to Dover sea front. In anticipation of the
event crowds started forming hours before the start. Some stayed on the
Sea Front to make sure of a good view of the clock bonfire, others flocked
to the Market Square or other vantage points along the route.

We decided to take up a position along Castle Street to view the procession as it left the Market Square and headed for the SeaFront. We could

hear the Mardi Gras music of the bands and the ripple of amazement and delight from the crowds long before the first section of the carnival reached us. Nothing had prepared us for the sheer extravagance and inventiveness in the depiction of the planets, each as splendid and colourful as the next; each with its own special theme, individual style of costume and its own high, sculptured standard bearer, leading each section. After the vivid red and orange colours of the sun, the nine planets each with its own distinctive colour coordination, passed us in turn, ending with the stark, black and white, skeleton-like depiction of Pluto. The mood of the carnival was of total celebration in the happy event, encouraging the thousands of spectators to join in with them, pulsating in time to the music. We marvelled at the amount of work which must have gone into the making of the elaborate costumes, in workshops all over the district which had started as early as October. The participants in the carnival were of all ages and from many organisations from Dover and from the surrounding villages.

As the procession passed, many of the onlookers joined the tail of it and followed it over Townwall Street and on to the promenade, which was so crowded it was impossible for latecomers to gain a vantage point to see

Carnival Procession on 1st January, 2000.

the Clock of the Third Millennium, which had risen out of the ashes of the old clock and awaited the arrival of the carnival. When all the sections of the Carnival of the Planets had reached the beach, the large mechanical structure of the clock was brought to life in a spectacle of lights, sound and pyrotechnic effects.

These had hardly died away when it was time for the start of a magnificent fireworks display, staged from the cliff top at Dover Castle and best viewed from the promenade. This must be one of the best displays ever seen in Dover and attracted one of the largest crowds for many years. As the tired but happy spectators made their way to homes or cars there was nothing but praise for the organisers and all who took part in the carnival.

We wish to record our thanks to:-

Derek Leach for his support and advice throughout the planning and production of the book and for his help with publicity and distribution.

May Jones and Derek Leach for proof-reading.

Elizabeth Owen of Dover Museum for her help in finding and tracing some of the pictures used in the book.

James Adams and the studio staff at Adams the Printers for technical assistance in the early stages.

Members of the Dover Society for their interest and encouragement.

PHOTOGRAPHS AND PICTURES:

We thank the following for their kind permission to reproduce photographs.

Dover Museum for three pictures of the Bronze Age Boat, the postcard of the Sea Front with bathing huts *circa* 1930, the pictures of the 'Golden Arrow; and the Marine Station and of the *'Glatton'* lying in Dover Harbour.

Dover Harbour Board for the picture of the *Royal Viking Sun.*

The Imperial War Museum for the pictures of defence measures on the Sea Front at East Cliff in World War II.

The *Times* newspaper and the Kent Messenger Group for the photographs of war damage in Wellesley Road and Liverpool Street.

Brian Petch for his painting of aircraft in the 1940s.

Andrew Jones for his two slides of cross-Channel boats.

The *Dover Express* for the three photographs of the Carnival Procession on 1st January, 2000.

The relatives of May Bradley for photographs from her scrap book.

Nan Wheeler for the photographs of the Minerva Orchestra and the house at Barham.

June Dyer for the photograph on Dover beach.

Eddie Clapson for his photograph of Ralph's School.

Merril Lilley provided the photographs of the cruise terminal, the S.E.C.R. war memorial and the terrace of houses at East Cliff. All other photographs in the book are from the collection of 'Budge' Adams.